THE
CAMDEN
MURDER

THE
CAMDEN TOWN MURDER

THE LIFE AND DEATH
OF
EMILY DIMMOCK

NEW AND REVISED EDITION

BY

JOHN BARBER

Published by
Mandrake of Oxford
PO Box 250
OXFORD
OX1 1AP (UK)

A CIP catalogue record for this book is available from the British Library and the US Library of Congress.

ISBN 9781869928148

CONTENTS

ILLUSTRATIONS

ACKNOWLEDGEMENTS

There could have been no book without Alan Stanley. We have corresponded by email, letter and phone and met just once but he has become a very good friend. I value his commitment, research and dedication no end.

Robert (Bob) Shaw passed on to me many family letters and contemporary newspaper reports without which many of the people mentioned in this book could never have become so well drawn.

Paul Brooks corresponded with me over a year or more, passing on medical and forensic notes and even copies of the police file. His expert assistance has allowed me to finish a book I never thought possible.

Miss Jean Overton Fuller for allowing me to use hitherto unpublished research.

Mogg Morgan at Mandrake for opening new doors.

And to countless researchers at the many newspapers and television stations who have kept making enquiries through my website and in doing so convinced me that the book was worth writing.

INTRODUCTION

On the morning of September 12, 1907 the body of Emily Dimmock was found in her rented rooms in Camden Town, North London. Her throat had been cut, almost to the point where her head was severed from her body. The murderer has never been identified.

This is the story of Emily's life; along with an account of the times in which she lived and the circumstances surrounding her death. A recent survey by Discovery Channel ranked the Camden Town Murder as Britain's third most famous unsolved murder after the Whitechapel killings of Jack the Ripper and The Peasenhall Mystery of 1902.

Robert Wood, a designer and artist was tried and acquitted of her murder. It is generally acknowledged that he was saved from the gallows following a brilliant defence conducted by Edward Marshall Hall QC.

This book traces Emily's short life from her birth in a small Hertfordshire village to her last days in rented rooms in Camden Town. It covers much of her family's history, and the lives of the many colourful characters from both sides of the legal divide that populate this mystery.

After almost two years of research into all aspects of the case including hitherto unpublished letters and correspondence; and with the benefit of modern forensic knowledge, a solution to this mystery may now have been found.

It is never easy after almost one hundred years to be able to state with absolute certainty that the murderer can be identified beyond any reasonable doubt. This book presents all the background and the evidence; the reader can make up their own mind as to whether this provides the proof that would have been sufficient for a conviction in 1907.

Writing this in 2004, it is frustrating not to be able to question the police investigation team, or the witnesses, or the friends and acquaintances of Emily Dimmock; and of Robert Wood. All that is available is written in police files, memoirs of some of the major players and oral recollections of family members now also departed but handed down to present generations along with fragments of letters and contemporary newspaper reports.

Yet throughout history there are echoes of characters and motives that haunt this mystery.

As the chapters unfold and Emily's life rushes to its terrible conclusion, many suspects step briefly into the spotlight, only to recede once more into the backstage shadows. And all the time the presence of Robert Wood is always there. At first just a description of a man without a name but once identified he dominates the investigation.

He was a graphic artist; a young man of undoubted and acknowledged ability who designed intricate patterns for etching on glass. He had talent, a good salary, youth, possessed of good looks and the admiration and respect of a wide circle of friends. How then, did someone so sensitive become embroiled in such a violent crime?

Comparisons reach out with other creative geniuses throughout the centuries for whom violence and violent death appear constant companions.

Carravaggio the sixteenth century Italian artist could create works of great elegance yet, almost all his works portrayed the dark side of Roman life. He spent his life one short step ahead of the legal process that could have condemned him to a life of imprisonment, involved in fights, street brawls and personal quarrels with friends and enemies alike.

Christopher Marlowe who many still consider Shakespeare's equal and some that he was the real author of the Shakespeare canon, was involved in a street fight in his early years in London before falling victim himself to a fatal stabbing.

In the 1960s, Joe Meek the record producer who launched the Tornados to fame with Telstar shot his landlady dead and then turned the gun on himself. It is thought that he had become enraged with jealousy after Heinz Burt, one of the Tornados founder members left him for a young girl.

Jealousy had accounted for a man that had done so much to forward British popular music in the mid-60s. It was the motive behind the death of another talented artist, the playwright Joe Orton. In the same year 1967, and in the same area of Holloway, North London, that Joe Meek put an end to his own life on the anniversary of the death of Buddy Holly, Joe Orton was bludgeoned to death by Kenneth Halliwell. Consumed with jealousy over the rising popularity and commercial success of his lover he then took his own life with an overdose of sleeping pills.

Many artists capable of dramatic and tender works appear to keep within them demons that are capable of unleashing terrible violence. None more so than in the central figure in the case of the Camden Town Murder. Underneath the respectable veneer of middle class Edwardian England typified by the gentle artist

Robert Wood, lay many entwined levels of corruption, privation, despair, unemployment and immorality.

Only lately has the murder of Emily Dimmock been linked with the Whitechapel murders and the enigmatic figure of Jack the Ripper. The connection is examined later in this book, and if we are to believe the words of at least one authority, Walter Sickert was so troubled by the murder of Mary Kelly that it haunted him all his life, and the Camden Town Murder series was his way of expiating the scene from his memory.

This is not another 'Ripper' book but, the effect of Emily's murder on one of Britain's leading artists seems to emphasise the thin walls that sometimes exist between art, artists and the darker side of man.

I am forever in the debt of Alan Stanley for introducing this case to me. He emailed me in April 2002, as a result of reading an article I had written on the Old Bedford Music Hall in Camden Town. 'You seem to know a lot about the history of the area. I am researching my family background and hope you might know something about the Camden Town Murder'.

This was the message Alan wrote and we spent many more months exchanging information. One of the most intriguing aspects of the case was the many co-incidences that kept occurring and more than once Alan wrote to me stating that if anyone was to write about this then it would have to be me.

At the time of her death Emily was living in St Pauls Road, close to Camden Town. It was renamed Agar Grove (as it is today) and when my parents married in 1940 they first rented rooms at 10, Agar Grove, almost opposite No 29 where Emily died. Emily's mother Sarah was born in Much Hadham, a very picturesque Hertfordshire village where I too lived for a year after leaving the City where I worked for 17 years.

There are many other such co-incidences that arose as I investigated further which are mentioned in the following pages. A little further into our correspondence, Alan mentioned that he had exchanged some information with a chap he had met through the *Family History Magazine*. The latter was also a retired Bank Manager and his name too was John Barber.

I had never heard of the Camden Town Murder, despite having lived close to the site for almost 30 years. My parents never mentioned it despite living for some time opposite the actual house, but once I began to read of the murder and of Emily's life I have been compelled to follow all leads I could find in an attempt to solve the case.

Much of what I have uncovered has been published on my website. The latter generated a huge amount of interest and many of the people who took time to write and comment or offer advice have been acknowledged wherever possible. I stopped updating the web pages and offering articles for publication once my research pushed me into a certain direction.

When I started this enquiry, I did not appreciate the huge interest in the Camden Town Murder. Much has been fanned by the interest taken by the American crime writer Patricia Cornwell. I could not write this book without some comment on her theories, nor on the part played if at all, by Walter Sickert. Therefore the Whitechapel murders form a brief chapter.

I hope the conclusion may bring a little peace to the relatives of those who found themselves caught up in this terrible crime.

1 EARLY LIFE

Standon

All contemporary reports and all the books that have included references to the Camden Town Murder have consistently referred to the victim as 'Phyllis' Dimmock. Although this is the name by which she asked to be called, her real name was Emily Elizabeth Dimmock and I shall refer to her as Emily throughout.

There have been many reports as to her place of birth, but it was Alan Stanley who first tracked down Emily's birth certificate, and this states that she was born on 20 October 1884 in The Village, Standon. Her mother Sarah, was at the time resident at the 'Red Lion', Standon.

Standon is a small village in Hertfordshire on the A120, between Bishops Stortford and the A10 trunk road between London and Cambridge. A mile past

Standon on the way to Bishops Stortford and Stanstead Airport, is a staggered crossroads known as Hadham Cross. Turning right here will lead you to Little Hadham and a little further on to Great Hadham, known these days as Much Hadham.

Both are quiet, picturesque English villages. Much Hadham has a long High Street, a couple of pubs and an antique shop that features quite regularly in UK TV period drama series. Sarah Dimmock was born in Great Hadham and was 42 at the time of Emily's birth. She already had 5 children, the eldest of which Rosa was also born in Great Hadham.

I live in Hertford which is close to Standon and the Hadhams and for a short while lived in Much Hadham itself so it was natural of Alan to ask me to verify the record. It was one of many coincidences that pepper this story.

The last remaining pub in Standon is the 'Bell'. It is a friendly, local village pub with a large beer garden, and hosts the annual May Day celebrations in the village with Morris Men and maypole dancing. I could find no reference to a pub called the 'Red Lion'.

In a newspaper report of 1907 (actual title unknown) published shortly after Emily's death, William her father confirmed this account: 'The father of William Dimmock who kept the "Shoulder of Mutton" was a brother of my father. I never kept a public house in

The Bell as it is today.

Emily Dimmock's Birth Certificate.

Hitchin; the only public house I kept was the "Red Lion" in Standon.'

In the middle of 2005, Alan Stanley came to visit me in Hertford, and on the way stopped off in Standon to experience for himself at first hand the genesis of this story. He tracked down an elderly resident who had heard mention of the 'Red Lion'; it is now called Peppers Cottage and is opposite the 'Bell'.

William Dimmock is listed in the 1881 Kelly's as a beer retailer. At this time there were ale houses which were licensed to sell ale or beer and were mostly somebody's living room; and public houses or inns which were much larger premises in which you could get a meal and possibly a bed.

William Dimmock was 37 when Emily was born. He gave his occupation as 'carpenter, journeyman'. In the census return of 1881 he states that he is a 'photographic artist'. At the time of the census the family were living in Lambeth, South London then a part of the county of Surrey. They had 4 children; Rosa aged 6, William aged 4, Esther Elizabeth aged 3, and Henry John aged 1. William is recorded as being born in Codicote which is on the north western side of Hertfordshire as Standon is on the east, and Esther and Henry born in Walworth and Lambeth respectively which are both districts in the same part of South London.

There was a fifth child born in 1883, Maud. Her

brothers and sisters had a great influence on Emily's life and it was Henry who was called to identify her body. At the time of her death, Henry and Rosa were in Luton, Maud was in Putney, South London and William in Smethwick in the Midlands.

Emily was William and Sarah's sixth child. In the same newspaper report quoted above William mentions that he lost two children whilst at Standon. All of his children can be accounted for in the 1901 census with the exception of Esther, so perhaps, either there was a child that had not been registered or at the time of the report he was unclear as to the past.

Whatever the truth they died in terrible circumstances – from hydrophobia or what we now know today as rabies. It was a more common cause of death than it is today. Ironically at the time Louis Pasteur was developing a vaccine against rabies which he had perfected by 1886, about the time of the Dimmock's loss. Rabies was common in open, rural woodland. Even today a drive through the countryside around Standon and the Hadhams is reminiscent of times when there were no cars, no motorways and little intensive farming.

Hitchin

The death of his children may have been the cause of William's departure. Little is known of their home life until about 1895 or 1896 when Emily was just 11. The family was living in Oakfield, Hitchin. Emily was out on Hitchin Hill pushing a pram (whose child within is not stated) when a horse bolted from its cart and knocked her over. She was taken to Hitchin Hospital.

More is known nowadays about head injuries and more care taken over the patient's recovery but even at the turn of the century Emily's injury was severe enough for her to be kept in hospital for three weeks. During her stay she was found wandering in the street by a local lad named Henry Turner who took her back to the hospital.

Her injury was indeed serious and William was told that 'she would either have to go to a lunatic asylum or be taken care of at home as the accident had affected her mind'. This was confirmed by her sister Rosa who had told the *Hitchin Express* that 'she had been knocked down by a horse on Hitchin Hill when she was 11 and it had affected her mind'[1]

In the absence of any medical reports it is not easy to know how seriously this accident had affected Emily's mind. Severe concussion can lead to headaches, tiredness and even depression. The condition can last for years and can result in a personality change or a loss or reduction in intellectual and reasoning abilities.

From his later comments William appears to be very protective of Emily. He states that for 'weeks and weeks I dragged her around in a bath chair until she seemed to get better'. This accident and its aftermath may account for Emily's later behaviour. A few years after the accident William became very angry over his daughter Maud interfering in Emily's life and it may be that in that very large family, only the father really understood what had happened to Emily.

I have already hinted at William's roving nature. His children were born in many different parts of southern England and his occupation appears to have changed almost as often as he changed address. From the interview already quoted the reporter gives this account of William Dimmock:

'It seems that Mr Dimmock, who is apparently an energetic, respectable man, has had a varied career. For 25 years he travelled England Ireland and Wales as an exhibitor of dissolving views in connection with the Church of England Zenana Mission and the Indian Normal School Instruction Society – as he described it. In this capacity, he has been the guest of many well known people. Then he started on his own account entirely, and for 20 miles around Hitchin he had given limelight entertainments at scores of villages. He says he still makes his 'Cough candy' and from his account of the trade done he must have a good connection at Wellingborough, where he still resides while visiting Hitchin market.'

This would explain his first remarks on the 1881 census as a photographic artist. He gave what we used to call 'magic lantern' shows. This was in the very early stages of photography, cinema was in its infancy and the major source of entertainment was still the pub and the music hall.

William Dimmock appears to have been a very religious man. The Zenana Bible and Medical Mission was founded by Lady Kinnaird who had heard of the conversion to Christianity of a high caste Indian woman.

A Zenana is a harem, and the Church of England Zenana Mission specialised in sending missionaries to educate and evangelise the women of such closed communities. Its main aim was to convert the women of India by means of normal schools (teacher training colleges), Zenana visiting, medical missions, Hindu and Muslim female schools and the employment of Bible women.

In 1852, Lady Kinnaird founded the London Board for the Calcutta Normal School which consisted of both male and female members but because of cultural restrictions only women missionaries were able to teach the local women in religious instruction. In 1880 the Board included medical aid in their work and it was on behalf of the Zenana Bible and Medical Mission that William gave talks and magic lantern shows.

Her father was obviously fond of Emily. Bert

Emily wearing a sailor's hat.
You can just make out 'Prince of Wales'.

Shaw's family recall many times that they visited Emily and himself. Emily entertained with singing but would not sing 'Ship Ahoy'; I have quoted the song below.

I was drifting away on life's pitiless sea,
And the angry waves threatened my ruin to be,
When away at my side, there I dimly descried,
A stately old vessel, and loudly I cried:
"Ship ahoy! Ship ahoy!"
And loudly I cried: "Ship ahoy!"

'Twas the "old ship of Zion," thus sailing
along,
All aboard her seemed joyous, I heard their
sweet song;
And the Captain's kind ear, ever ready to hear,
Caught my wail of distress, as I cried out in
fear:
"Ship ahoy! Ship ahoy!"
As I cried out in fear: "Ship ahoy!"

The good Captain commanded a boat to be
low'red,
And with tender compassion He took me on
board;
And I'm happy today, all my sins washed away
In the blood of my Savior, and now I can say:
"Bless the Lord! Bless the Lord!"

The Swan Hotel as it is today.

From my soul I can say: "Bless the Lord!"
O soul, sinking down 'neath sin's merciless
wave,
The strong arm of our Captain is mighty to
save;
Then trust Him today, no longer delay,
Board the old ship of Zion, and shout on your
way:
"Jesus saves! Jesus saves!"
Shout and sing on your way: "Jesus saves!"

We can only guess at the reasons for Emily's reluctance to sing this. Did it remind her of her father and his beliefs, and the disgrace she had brought on him, or was it a painful reminder of her relationship with Henry Biddle. This is a photo of Emily wearing a sailor's cap – Biddle was a member of the crew on the HMS Prince of Wales, but more of him later.

Whether Emily made a complete recovery from that fall or not is unknown. Her sister Rosa confirmed that she continued to attend St Mary's School, Hitchin until she was 13.

Bedford

About 1898-1899, William moved to Bedford. Emily would have been about 14 and she went to work at the Swan Hotel in Bedford. William goes on to state that she eventually became chief chambermaid. In April

1899 she was still in Hitchin as Rosa states that she 'nursed me in my confinement.'

Emily's movements about this time become a little unclear. The 1901 census states that she was in service in St Neots as a domestic servant aged 16, but was apparently back in Bedford in 1902, perhaps re-employed by Mr Swan at his hotel in her improved position.

Kings Cross

Sometime that year Emily's life took a dramatic turn. This is the story according to her father: 'One day while I was away from Bedford my daughter Maud, now the wife of a police constable at Putney, came over on a visit and took Emily back to London with her without my permission. Yes she took her to Finchley. That was her first place in London, and now she is buried there.'

Maud was then 19 and by 1907, at the time of Emily's murder had become Mrs Maud Coleman. In 1902, the huge rise in the number of domestic servants and large households seen at the height of the Victorian era, was beginning to decline. The thrill of a move to London might have been just too much to dismiss for a young girl tempted by the talk of bright lights from her elder sister.

Emily appears to have remained in service for a number of years although returning to Hitchin in

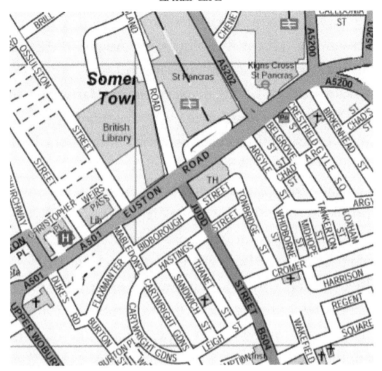

Many of the streets still exist — 2, Grafton Place (1904), 65 Harrison Street, 5 Upper Chadwell Street, 60 Burton Crescent (all 1905), 12 Belgrave Street, 121 Judd Street, 1 Bidborough Street, 13 Manchester Street, 28 Gower Place and then back to 2 Grafton Place (in 1906).

1903, at the request of her brother Henry, but no reason is given for this request. In August 1904, she visited her sister Rosa then living in Luton. Rosa was already married having the surname of Martindale. In 1901, she was working in the straw hat industry, a local trade for which Luton has become famous – the local football team's nickname is the Hatters.

Emily may already have been experiencing some problems in her life for a week later she asked Rosa if she could stay with her. Rosa agreed and found her work at Richard Burley's factory in the Old Bedford Road. When work dried up, Emily was forced to pawn her clothes but stayed on in the November of 1904, to nurse Rosa through what appears to be the birth of another child.

William Dimmock was at that time also living in Luton. He later recalled visiting Rosa and stating that the only possessions left in Emily's box were her Prayer Book and Bible. William then moved to Northampton and in June of 1907, to Wellingborough where he was living at the time of Emily's death.

But in December 1904, Emily suddenly ran away to London again; this time in the company of a Lucy Martindale who might possibly have been Rosa's sister-in-law, as in 1907, she refers to her as Mrs Dowset. The latter had also fallen on hard times as she was an inmate of the Luton Union, or workhouse.

During the next couple of years, Emily made some

brief visits to her sister and told Rosa in 1905, that she was earning a living as a dressmaker. Ivy Shaw, Bert's sister recalls: 'Emily was a very clever girl. I remember seeing Emily at a machine making Bert a silk scarf.'

No one really knows what happened to Emily during those years presumably spent in London. However, the police investigation uncovered evidence that as early as 1904, when not quite 20, Emily was already living the life of a prostitute in Luton. She had begun to meet trouble head on.

This is the report from DC Joseph Henry Attwood of Borough Police Office, Luton, on 16 September 1907, to his Chief Constable which was submitted to the Officer in Charge of the case in London:

'I have to report to you for your information that about two years ago (1905) a man named Summock and his wife resided in this Town, and he was employed by a local straw hat manufacturer. At that time he was cohabiting with the murdered girl Dimmock, who was staying here at the time. Summock's wife found them together in the Churchyard, and she gave him a black eye. Shortly after he went with his wife and took a licensed house in a short road just off Grays Inn ('the Edgware' crossed through) Road, Camden Town end, and he was residing at this house about a fortnight ago. I am unable to get the sign of the house.'

This short report contains all the future elements of Emily's life – even to the Grays Inn Road area of North London.

About this time two other men entered Emily's life. In early 1906, she again visited Rosa. This time in the company of a girl named Annie and a soldier. He was a large man – over 6' 3" with dark hair and eyebrows and according to Rosa, piercing eyes. This was 'Jumbo' Hurst, a private in the Grenadier Guards, stationed at Tower Hill. Perhaps Emily had succumbed to 'scarlet fever', a slang term for poor servant girls attracted by the glamour of the soldier's red uniform. The soldier in turn could extract sexual favours cheaper than buying them on the streets.

When the list of suspects was being drawn up, he was vividly recalled by Rosa who I believe took an instant dislike to the man. Not much more was heard of 'Jumbo' until after the murder but another man had entered Emily's life.

This was the sailor Henry or Harry Biddle. Rosa recalls receiving two letters from Biddle in late 1906, claiming that he and Emily had married and living in Portsmouth, and asking if she could let them two rooms. Rosa agreed but heard no more. The two letters appear to have been destroyed by the police but their investigations in Portsmouth uncovered no evidence that a marriage had taken place.

The police investigation was indeed exhaustive. In their pursuit of the murderer the team located all Emily's known London addresses from 1904 to 1907. All of them were within a couple of hundred yards of each other and all within close proximity to the Euston Road, the popular haunt for prostitutes around Kings Cross, St Pancras and Euston stations with the many bars on every corner and side street.

It was at 1, Bidborough Street, and up until his arrest for keeping a disorderly house at 13, Manchester Street, that Emily came into contact with John William Crabtree, horse thief and general low life who served a couple of terms of hard labour. He was the only other man in Emily's life who had a cast iron alibi at the time of her murder. He was in prison. John Crabtree knew the Kings Cross area well and many of the men that knew Emily. He was to become a vital witness in the investigation.

By the end of 1906 or beginning of 1907, Emily was living at 50, Great (now Royal) College Street, and met Bert Shaw. Her life was about to change.

Notes

1   *Lust, Dust and Cobblestones* - Sue Fisher.

2 MURDER!

Bert Shaw

Bertram John Eugene Shaw was born in 1888. This was as Alan Stanley said, an auspicious date. It was the year of Jack the Ripper, and a little coincidental that the Camden Town Murder has since been linked to the Whitechapel murderer.

Bert left home at the age of 15, which was not unusual for lads at that time, and secured a job as a chef at Leicester with the Midland Railway. Later he was based at St Pancras where he worked on the Sheffield Express.

According to the family he met Emily when he was 18, probably late 1906 or early 1907, which ties in with Emily's change of address.

Where they met is pure conjecture. In his book *The Camden Town Murder* which is a part fictionalised account of the events leading up to the trial and beyond, Sir David Napley suggests that they could have met at, or close to, St Pancras station. This is not improbable. Bert's family were living and still do, in Northampton and there is also a chance that they could have met during one of Emily's trips home.

Whatever the details of their early affair, Bert soon moved into 50, Great College Street. In today's climate, they would have appeared to all outward appearances a normal couple living together. Such a loose arrangement was not so acceptable in Edwardian society, and they were living as Mr and Mrs Shaw, which were the names on the rent book.

Bert had already introduced Emily to his family. She had stayed at the family home in Moore Street and shared a bedroom with Ethel another of Bert's sisters.

In 1907, minors, young people under the age of 21, were not allowed to marry without their parents consent – the giving of the consent was registered on the marriage certificate. They had not been together for very long before deciding on marriage for in early 1907 Bert's parents had received the official papers for their consent.

Some surviving members of Bert's family believe that this consent was withheld by his mother. His sister Ivy writes in a letter to her nephew: 'Afterwards Mother and Dad received papers for Bert to sign being under age for marriage. Dad refused to sign, but later on mother persuaded him to sign but as you now know they were living together.'

The Shaw family appear to have accepted Emily and been quite fond of her. Ivy recalls spending a holiday with Emily and Bert in London and going along to the 'Old Bull and Bush' a popular pub in Hampstead immortalised in the music hall song. Emily's machine skills and singing have already been mentioned above.

The unanswered question is to whether the Shaw's knew anything of Emily's life in London. I don't believe so. At least not until after the murder when the police investigation uncovered so much of Emily's past.

William Dimmock doesn't believe so either. In the interview with the newspaper referred to above he adds: 'Yes, and strange to say, while I was in Northampton she was visiting Shaw's parents – nice people. They were getting ready, so Mrs Shaw told me to get married, and Mrs Shaw had a paper which her husband signed for the purpose of them getting married, because their son was under-age. This son has worked himself up to a good position as a chef on the Midland Railway, and Mrs Shaw had no idea about Emily's life.'

This visit must have been in August 1907, for William continues: 'I tried my utmost to ascertain Emily's whereabouts, but none of the brothers or

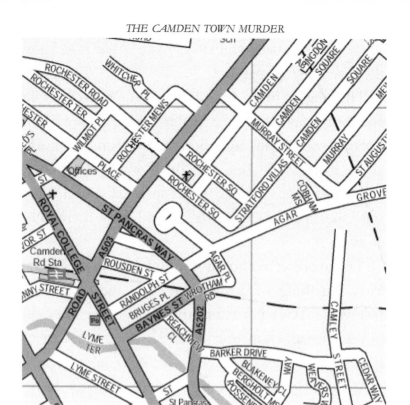

Map of the St Pauls Road (Agar grove) area.

sisters would let me know. Many residents at Northampton can prove that Emily was at Northampton last August making anxious enquiries for her father and mother there. Could God have sent it that she had found us! This dreadful blow would never have happened.'

There can be no way of understanding William's grief. He seems to be blaming himself and his own family. There is no reason for his family withholding details of Emily's whereabouts, unless they too were trying to protect him, he being also innocent of her life until it was too late.

The other person who must have known of Emily's lifestyle was Bert himself. Many previous accounts (probably based on Napley's book) have tried to suggest that Bert convinced Emily to give up her life on the streets and accept the normal conventions of marriage. It is unlikely. Emily was most probably carrying on her past trade as a prostitute with more than just a 'nod' from Bert.

It is not an attitude to be scorned. Life was not easy for the average working class couple, especially those that aspired to the better things in life. To secure that life, certain sacrifices had to be made, and accepting the fact that your wife had to sell her body in return for extra cash was part of that deal. Once the police began to investigate Bert and Emily's background and finances, it was evident that they were living well

Robert Wood, from a drawing by Joseph Simpson.

beyond their means, and could not have been solely dependent on Bert's earnings from the railway for their livelihood.

Bert's initial wage of seventeen shillings a week was well below the average of a guinea or £1.1shilling (£1.05 in decimal currency). Amongst their possessions were a piano and sewing machine. In common with many of their contemporaries they aspired to the trappings of a middle class lifestyle.

The rising middle classes were beginning to embrace the concept of mobility and moving out to the 'green lungs' such as Hampstead Garden Suburb. Bert and his landlord Mr Stocks walked to the nearby rail stations where they worked, and as this story unfolds more examples are presented of a working class tied to their community, never more than a short walk from their place of employment.

There was a different kind of mobility for the working classes; often moving no more than a few streets away to escape rent arrears or the tally man; or the debt collector representing hire purchase companies as he might be described today.

In the middle of 1907, the couple were on the move again, still living as Mr and Mrs Shaw, and exhibiting their rent book as proof of their respectability. They moved from 50 Great College Street, to No 21, and then for a couple of weeks in early June to 27 St

Pancras Square. Finally they moved into two rooms at 29 St Pauls Road, the home of Mr and Mrs Stocks.

Mr Stocks worked on the railways; as did so many characters in this story. He was up early and consequently went to bed early. As did Mrs Stocks who protested that she had no idea that the nice couple upstairs, especially 'Mrs Shaw' were leading an immoral life and using her house as a place for entertaining clients.

She was not alone. She most probably turned a blind eye to what was happening, as long as the rent was paid and none of the neighbours suspected anything. For most people at the turn of the century in working class London, it was a matter of getting by at whatever cost.

Emily appeared content. She was living with a good man who worked hard and kept her as best he could. She had a piano and a sewing machine and the company of her many friends in the pubs of North London, especially the 'Rising Sun' in Euston Road and the 'Eagle' in Great College Street.

Every afternoon at about 4.15pm Bert left for work, to return home the next morning at about 11.30am. It allowed her to go out at night and drink with her mates, and meet the many men that were happy to pay for an overnight stay at 29 St Pauls Road, and be smuggled in when the Stocks had retired to bed before another early morning.

Robert Wood

There were many men in her life, but one special male friend was known to all of her acquaintances although few knew his name. This was Robert William Thomas George Cavers Wood

In 1907 Robert Wood was living with his father and half brother James George Wood at 12, Frederick Street, just off the Grays Inn Road, Kings Cross. On the death of his mother Margaret Cavers in 1880, the family moved down south from Edinburgh where his father George Wood, found work as a printers compositor. He re-married but his second wife also passed away in the early part of 1907.[1]

Robert went to the Thanet Church School in St Pancras. He was a popular student with no outstanding recognisable talent. However he found work at the Australian Medical Students Club as an assistant steward. This social club was part of the University College of London that was situated in Gower Street. It was founded in 1826, and offered many courses in the sciences and medical disciplines.

It was here that he discovered his talent for sketching. Students were eager for his drawings from medical textbooks, and it is possible that from this work he gained a reputation for his artistic skills. This application soon repaid him. Although the Club was closed in 1893 he found employment better suited to these talents.

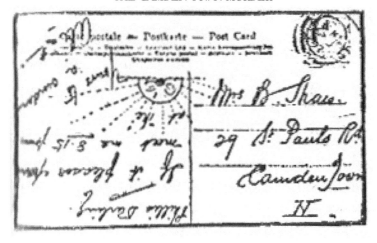

Emily Dimmock received this postcard.
Could it have been sent by her murderer?

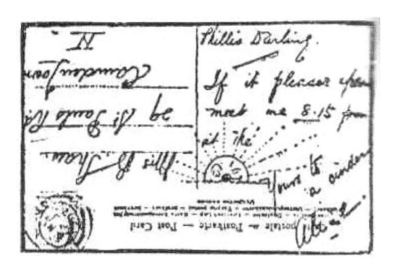

By 1907, when 30, he had been employed for many years by the Sand and Blast Manufacturing Company of Grays Inn Road to design figures and patterns for glassware.

There is no available documented evidence as to Robert Wood's training but this places him at the height of the popularity in Art Nouveau. The movement began in the late 1880s, and was at its peak whilst he was employed in Grays Inn Road. It was at a time when industrialisation had not just brought into being the huge mass of working class, but offered the opportunity for the mass production of household artefacts.

The industrialists and rising middle classes who were the benefactors of this newly created wealth developed a strong interest in things of beauty with which to decorate their homes, and there was no shortage of manufacturers or retailers to feed this hunger.

One of the founders of the Art Nouveau movement John Ruskin strongly advocated a return to craftsmanship, and a break from the rigid lines dividing fine art and decorative art. It was his major disciple William Morris who by founding Morris & Co was instrumental in bridging the gap, and employed artists to decorate cabinets, furniture, fabrics, chairs and a whole gamut of household and public wares.

The movement found its inspiration from nature;

from plants, flowers such as lilies, the plumage of peacocks and the fantastical shapes of dragonflies. It was a style that accentuated fluidity of line, liquidity and elegance, and found delight in the shapes and curves of the female form and from their flowing hair, curls and waves.

Many of the famous names worked with glass; Galle, Tiffany and Lalique. It was the invention of electric light, and the diverse and myriad patterns it imparted to glass that made that substance of great significance.

The name of the Sand and Blast Manufacturing Company evokes images of an industrial society and 'dark satanic mills'. This is an unfair comparison. Glass items were decorated by the sandblasting method, by which a special type of sand is blown through a funnel imitating a sand storm effect. The glass item would have been covered in masking tape around stencils, and sand blasted onto the exposed surface. When the stencil was removed the pattern would remain, uncovering layers of varying depth and opacity to fully explore the properties of the glassware itself.

Robert Wood had found the outlet for his artistic nature. The Art Nouveau movement may well have inspired him to produce designs of great detail and delicate line. There is no way of knowing from where he found his own personal inspiration. As can be seen above the female form was highly admired within the movement, and it was within the working class women of Kings Cross that Robert Wood was often found.

The poem 'Jenny' is quoted in more detail later on, but here are a few lines which also underline its significance to the story and to Wood's motivation.

Why, Jenny, as I watch you there,—
For all your wealth of loosened hair,
Your silk ungirdled and unlac'd
And warm sweets open to the waist,
All golden in the lamplight's gleam,—

Here is the contradiction that was Robert Wood. By day he was a skilled designer, admired and respected by his employers and colleagues. He was to all outward appearances a respectable, middle class man who was at home with all things beautiful.

But by night he became a different person. In command of a good salary and of pleasant but not outstanding looks, he frequented the pubs around Kings Cross, associating with the prostitutes and loose women that haunted the bars. And in one of these bars he met Emily Dimmock.

Many of Emily's acquaintances, including John Crabtree would testify that they had seen Robert Wood in her company for many years prior to 1907. Wood testified on oath that the first time he met Emily was on the night of Friday September 6th in the 'Rising

Sun', Euston Road. Whatever the truth of his initial association, the events leading up to Emily's murder can be said to have been put in motion on that night, and the chain of evidence began to be forged.

What is not in doubt is that on that Friday evening Emily met Robert Wood. And he made an appointment to meet her the following Monday. It was the manner of his invitation that was to form a major plank in the prosecution's case.

Emily was fond of postcards; she kept an album in their rooms at St Pauls Road. Wood was an accomplished artist. These two elements forged a link between them.

Wood pulled a postcard from his pocket. On one side was a sentimental picture of a woman with a child. On the other he wrote: 'Phillis Darling, If it pleases you, meet me at 8.15 at the (and here he drew a sketch of a rising sun) . Yours to a cinder. Alice.'

It has been assumed that he signed the card 'Alice', so as to disguise himself and to provide Emily with an innocent reason for receiving the card, supposedly from a girlfriend. Whatever the reasons the card was not sent until late the next Sunday or early hours of Monday 9th September.

It became a famous postcard, published in all the nations newspapers when the police investigation team began to search for the author.

Emily received the postcard and kept the appointment at the 'Rising Sun' in the Euston Road. This had been one of her favourite pubs when living in the area and somewhere sure to meet with other ladies that she knew.

Robert Roberts

Wood was not the only man to get Emily's attention. In the 'Rising Sun' that evening were two sailors on leave. One was Frank Clarke, the other Robert Percival Roberts, a ship's cook. He told the police that he saw Emily with another man early in the evening, of about 27/28 years of age, about 5' 7" in height, sallow complexion, dark hair and eyes, clean shaven, and dressed in a blue serge suit and bowler hat. They left together and returned but he left her about midnight.

Roberts went home with Emily that night. He had already been to Emily's house on the previous evening, and was to return once again to Emily's rooms on the next evening – Tuesday.

On the Wednesday morning, Emily received two letters and for this we only have Roberts evidence. One was a circular from a tailor and the other a letter which Emily showed to him. She informed him it came from the man she had seen in the 'Rising Sun', that it was making an appointment for that night at the 'Eagle' public house, Camden Town, that she was afraid of the man, but she would have to meet him, although she would rather not.

He saw a portion of the letter written in blue copying pencil on what appeared to be paper torn from a pocket book. Roberts recollection of this was that it read something like: 'Dear Phyllis – will you meet me at the Eagle, 8.30 tonight – Bert.'

According to Roberts, Emily then showed him the 'Rising Sun' postcard, and asked him to agree that the handwriting on both letters was identical. For whatever reason, Emily retained the postcard, but after stating that she must not leave it lying about in case her 'husband' should see it, she lit a match and set fire to the letter, and threw it in the fire-place.

Roberts expected to meet Emily again on the Thursday evening at the 'Rising Sun', and waited there drinking with his friend Frank Clarke. Emily did not show. She had kept that appointment at the 'Eagle'.

There are so many 'Roberts', 'Bobs' and 'Berts'; but as I said this case is littered with co-incidences.

September 11th

Whoever may have written the letter, Emily was seen in the Eagle with Robert Wood. Mrs Stocks – the landlady of 29 St Pauls Road – made a statement that Emily was in the habit of going out nightly and returned home after they had gone to rest. On the

The Eagle public house seen from Camden Road,
then and now.

night of the murder she left the house as usual about 8.30 or 9.00pm.

The 'Eagle' stood on the corner of Great College Street and Camden Road. A pub still stands there although it is now called 'Mac's Bar' and before that an attempt to cash in on the Irish theme craze when it was briefly 'Rosie O'Grady's'. The 'Eagle' was a large two bar pub with high ceilings, cigarette stained embossed wallpaper on the ceilings and engraved windows. It was typical of an Edwardian pub. It survived in its original state until the late 1990s.

In 1907, it must have been as welcome as a fire in winter with plenty of tables and chairs, cigarette smoke and a piano.

It was Emily's local. It is a short walk from St Pauls Road, over the rail tracks that snake into Kings Cross goods yard and St Pancras, and then under the railway bridge of the North London Line. Just past this bridge is a small alley in which a modern block of flats has been built. It is called Bruges Place. Robert Wood had spent a few weeks in Bruges earlier in 1907, just after the death of his stepmother although I doubt if the local Council had this fact in mind when they came to name the street.

Various friends and acquaintances of Emily testified to seeing her at the 'Eagle' pub. She was not dressed as one meeting a lover - her hair was still in curling papers, but much later on and in court Wood could not

Bruges Place

remember any details of her dress. By chance an old friend of Wood's, Joseph Lambert called into the pub and recalls Wood being with Emily. The last person to see them together was the barmaid, a Miss Raven who recalled Emily and Wood leaving at about 9.30pm.

It was the last time Emily was seen alive.

September 12th

On the morning of 12th September everything else was normal. However, Bert Shaw's mother had made arrangements to visit the couple. It was her first visit to London and she had travelled alone.

As stated above, Bert's working day meant that he would not finish until after 11.00am, so it would appear that arrangements had been made for Emily to meet her at Euston station. After waiting for a while she asked directions of a policeman and made her way to St Pauls Road.

She received no answer at the front door, but eventually was let in by Mrs Stocks who sat her down in the hallway.

Members of the Shaw family recollect that it was Mrs Shaw, standing on the steps of 29 St Pauls Road, who peered into the ground floor window and could see Emily lying on the bed. This is not impossible but highly improbable. I lived in a similar house to No29, as did many of my friends when we were growing up in that area. You can't actually see into the room through the glass and curtains; not without trying to break your neck. That is not to say that Mrs Shaw did not try. Ivy Shaw goes on to say that it was Bert who looked through the window. He may have done to check out the situation. Certainly Bert had no keys of his own, or not in his possession at the time.

As you enter through the front door there are two large rooms on your right or left depending on which side of the semi-detached you lived in. There is a long passageway running alongside these rooms and a staircase leading down to the basement. There is also a hallway at the foot of the stairwell, and presumably this is where Mrs Shaw sat awaiting Bert.

There have been many accounts of the discovery of Emily's body. The following is paraphrased from Inspector Arthur Neil's report of 8th October 1907, and must be considered to be as accurate a description of the events just prior to the discovery and of the murder scene.

Bert arrived home at his usual time, and was told by his mother that she could get no answer to her knocks. He was not surprised by this as he was under the impression that she had gone to meet his mother, and presumed that they had missed each other.

He borrowed a key from the landlady Mrs Stocks with which he opened the door of the front parlour, which Emily and he used as a sitting room.

The back room was used as a bedroom and

29 St Pauls Road, as it is today.

communicated with the front by means of folding doors. These Bert also found locked. He forced them and found Emily lying dead in the bed with her throat cut; the body covered only by the bed clothes.

His mother and Mrs Stocks entered the room with him; they immediately left, horrified at the spectacle, leaving everything as they had found it.

Bert went outside and found PC Thomas Killion, who was on duty close by in Camden Square, and he arrived at the house at 11.55am. This according to Ivy Shaw was the same policeman that had directed Mrs Shaw to the house earlier.

Emily was dead and cold and there were no signs of a struggle. PC Killion at first thought it was a case of suicide but he advised Somers Town Police Station and PS Toseland and subsequently Inspector Hufflet arrived.

Dr Thompson the Divisional Surgeon was sent for and on examining the body concluded that it was murder.

He was followed very shortly by Inspector Vady and Inspector Neil. Emily was lying on her left side slightly on her stomach, perfectly nude; her left cheek was resting on the pillow and her left arm was drawn across her back almost at right angles. Her right arm was stretched forward across the pillow, both hands clenched, her legs resting in a natural position as would be found in a person asleep, drawn slightly towards the trunk.

Her throat had been cut from ear to ear, the gash extending about six inches; the windpipe being almost completely severed. The cut was clean and had evidently been caused by a very sharp and strong instrument.

The only traces of the assailant was some blood-stained water in the wash-hand basin, and stains on a white cotton petticoat on which the hands had been wiped and then dipped in water.

In the front room, was a chest of drawers which had been pulled out and the drawers placed on the floor, the contents – mostly clothing – were scattered about the room, as if the murderer had been searching for something. The shutters of the room, which were generally fastened at night, had been pulled half open, and beside this everything in the room was in its normal position except a postcard album and its contents which were strewn about the floor.

From this description, it is unlikely that Bert or even Mrs Shaw could have seen Emily's body, or the bedroom.

Emily's body was removed and the investigation under Inspector Neil begun in earnest.

Notes

1   This amendment to my original draft was by courtesy of Michael Cotgrove who emailed me with much background to Robert Wood. He stated that 'Robert Wood's mother (Margaret Cavers) died in 1880 when he was 3 years old. Robert Wood was born in 1877, so in 1907 he was aged 30, not 28.'

The census for 1901 gives Robert's age as 25, which confirms this information.

3 THE INVESTIGATION

The scene of crime

At the end of the trial Inspector Neil wrote; 'The case was a most difficult and complicated one …. And my task an arduous one.'

There can be no doubt that Neil's investigations were exhaustive and as comprehensive as any murder enquiry could have been. The file at the Public Record Office is over 1400 pages thick and a testimony to the effort of the officers involved, notwithstanding the background of the victim. As soon as the investigation begun Emily's life was laid bare for all to criticise.

The first person to be eliminated was Bert Shaw. Enquiries made at St Pancras Station proved beyond any doubt that he was in Sheffield on the night of the murder, and did not reach London again until 10.45 am on the 12th.

Oddly, Ivy Shaw states that Bert was on a train running from London to Derby, not Sheffield, and had spent the night there. Derby was the headquarters of the Midland Railway as it was then, and the line continued and terminated at Sheffield. This was never questioned, and yet at the trial Edward Marshall Hall QC gave the impression that Bert could have somehow committed this crime. Just as swiftly as he planted the idea in the jury's head he withdrew it; but the implication has haunted the family ever since.

Poor Bert was first on the scene and one can only surmise his horror at finding Emily so brutally murdered.

In the twenty first century the room would have been scrutinised down to the finest detail. Fingerprints taken as well as blood samples and DNA. None of this was available in 1907. Bert's razors were visible close to the wash basin but it was never established that an old fashioned cut-throat razor could have been the murder weapon. Nor for that matter the actual weapon used. This is discussed in greater detail in a later chapter.

The attacker had wiped their hands on Emily's petticoat and this would have given a modern detective plenty of evidence to match the killer's profile. But this was 1907.

Two other details were noted by the Police Surgeon. Emily had sexual intercourse before her death and that although she had been infected by syphilis she was not suffering from that disease at the time of her death. DNA samples from her body would have been enough to identify her killer, but even this is still a relatively new science.

The one thing that Dr Thompson was able to confirm was that death had occurred at 3.00am. This was deduced from her body temperature and the onset of rigor mortis, and the remains of a light meal in her stomach. This was to become the cornerstone of Marshall Hall's defence.

Both Inspector Neil and Dr Thompson concluded that Emily had known her attacker well. She was completely naked, having had sex and drifted into sleep. Whilst in a state of repose her throat had been cut.

As can be seen earlier, Emily was well used to sneaking lovers into her rooms, past the early to bed Stocks. She must have been secure in the company of her killer to have had sex and then drifted into sleep. There were no other defensive knife marks on her body.

To cut someone's throat requires skill. To be as successful as Emily's killer the victim has to be asleep, or immobilised or very unprepared as once the victim starts to struggle then the chances of a very clean cut are diminished. In addition there is plenty of evidence of defensive cuts on the arms and upper torso. This type of murder is not common.

It was part of the ritual of the Whitechapel murders but the Ripper went on to completely mutilate the victims. The cut to Emily's throat may have given rise to speculation that Emily was a Ripper victim but along with the amount of time that had elapsed, almost 19 years, there were no other similarities. However, the possibility was raised by the American crime writer Patricia Cornwell and the implications are discussed in a separate chapter later in this book.

Suspect No.1 — Robert Roberts

Once Bert's alibi had been confirmed, suspicion fell on the ship's cook, Roberts. Neil began making enquiries in Emily's normal haunts, and that night met him at the 'Rising Sun'. He had been discharged from his ship in Swansea on 30th August and after reaching London, took up lodgings at the Euston Temperance Hotel, 173 – 5 Euston Road.

Roberts confirmed that he had spent the Sunday, Monday and Tuesday nights with Emily, and had crept out of the house at about 7.30am the following mornings. The manager at the Temperance Hotel also confirmed that Roberts had returned to his lodgings at about midnight on the night of the 11th September. However, Roberts must have known that he was certainly considered as a chief suspect, and recounted to Neil the events of the Wednesday morning when Emily had shown him the letter and postcard.

On hearing this, Neil organised a further search of Emily's room and found a charred letter in the grate. The actual message was unclear and both defence and prosecution barristers were able to put their own different interpretations on it. Roberts stuck to his own story as to its content. It was in his interests to deflect blame and described to Neil the man that he had seen with Emily on the previous Monday evening – the night for which the appointment on the postcard had been made.

So began the hunt for the man in the blue serge suit.

At this stage, Roberts was Neil's only means of identifying the stranger. Roberts remained in London to assist Neil, and at various occasions Neil applied for funds from the Police Information Fund to repay Roberts for his time.

'He has been rendering us very great assistance' wrote Neil on 10 October, when applying for a further £4, after an initial £3 had been paid on his request dated 18 September. This total payment of £7.00 would amount to about £450 today. Bert Shaw was earning about 18 shillings a week in 1907, so that Roberts was receiving an average weekly wage for the weeks leading up to the trial. 'Very great assistance' indeed.

There has been a suspicion in most people's minds

that Roberts could have been the killer. This would have made him a very cool customer indeed. Similar occurrences are not uncommon, even today. Roberts stayed in London although by profession a sailor, and continued to help the police by attending identification parades and accepting financial assistance. I believe that a guilty man might well have returned back to sea as soon as the crime was committed, rather than hang about in the pocket of a London detective.

Roberts, well aware that he remained a chief suspect, took out an insurance policy. He gave himself an alibi in the form of a female acquaintance May Campbell. Her evidence was a concoction of lies and she was lucky not to be charged with wasting police time. It was Marshall Hall's junior, Wellesley Orr who spotted the collaboration between Roberts and Campbell but the prosecution had already decided not to call her as a witness.

This is a little ahead of the early days in the investigation. There were other people in the 'Rising Sun' that Monday night who saw Emily with the stranger. He was no stranger to them at all, having been seen in the pub on and off for a couple of years.

Suspect No 2 — The man in the blue serge suit
They were Frank Clarke, Florence Smith of 16 Arlington Road and Mrs Lawrence of 16 Arlington St, Barnsbury (both prostitutes), and Edward Smyth a

barman at the 'Rising Sun'. They confirmed Roberts description of a man aged about 26, 5ft 7 or 8 in height, of dark sallow complexion, sunken eyes, dark hair, of rather morose appearance, with quite a noticeable number of pimples on his chin and lower part of face. To the best of Roberts belief he was clean shaven and was dressed in a dark, or blue serge suit with a rather old fashioned felt hat.

Whilst Roberts was there drinking, a man entered the bar about 8.30pm and remained there about three quarters of an hour in close conversation with Emily. They appeared to be having an argument. Then they both left, but returned till about 11pm and remained till about 11.45pm when they again went out. Emily returned alone about midnight and said to some of her women acquaintances 'I have made it all right with him. I have promised to meet him another night.'

Further statements were taken in the area, one from a window cleaner named Albert Miller. He had known Emily for about two years prior to her death. About a year previous, he was in the 'Rising Sun' with a Grenadier Guardsman known as Jumbo who was very friendly with Emily at the time. Emily looked scared when a man answering to Roberts description looked into the bar.

She went out to him followed by Jumbo who also went outside looking to fight the man. Miller persuaded

Jumbo to come in. He did so and the other man ran away.

Miller was later called to an identification parade to see if he could remember the man who ran away. He did.

Obviously this was the same 6' 3" appropriately named 'Jumbo' Hurst that Emily took to Luton to meet her sister Rosa. The police appeared to make some effort in locating him, ascertaining that he was now married and stationed at the Tower of London. He hadn't been seen in the neighbourhood for some time and he was dropped from further enquiries.

Suspects Nos 3 & 4 — Harrap and Woods

As Neil's enquiries continued more names surfaced. Bert Shaw may have been understandably reluctant to offer the names of any of Emily's male friends, but he did mention those of a Harrap who lived in Camden Town, and a Bert Woods, a fellow attendant on the restaurant cars of the Midland Railway.

Harrap had been known to have uttered unspecified threats against Emily. Neil traced him to 61 Arlington Road. He made a statement, and gave a sample of his handwriting which did not match that found on the charred remains of the latter. His alibi was checked and Neil was certain he was not in Emily's company on the night of her murder.

Bert Woods was found to be William Herbert

Woods. On the night of the murder, he reached London about 10.30pm, finished his work, and spent the rest of the evening playing billiards at the 'Golden Lion' public house, Kings Cross. Woods was seen and heard to arrive at his lodgings in Leighton Road, Kentish Town, by a fellow lodger at 1.30am.

Although it is not clear what exact threats Harrap used against Emily, he was not the only man to treat her like this. Many of her acquaintances had good cause to wish her harm, for many of them claimed to have caught venereal disease from her.

Neil discovered that Emily had been admitted to the Lock Hospital on 16th March 1905. The London Lock Hospital was founded in 1746, by William Bromfield. It was the first voluntary hospital for venereal diseases, but after being taken over by the National Health Service in 1948, it was closed in 1953. The hospital was originally at Grosvenor Place, near Hyde Park until 1841. In 1842, it moved to Harrow Road, Westbourne Grove. A new building was opened in 1862, at Dean Street, and Harrow Road became 'The Female Hospital.' Dean Street was for male out-patients.

It will be remembered that about this time, the Luton Police reported that she was already living an immoral life, and a little while later, was cohabiting with a man called Summock who also moved into the Kings Cross area of North London.

Emily could have contracted the disease at any time, and although clear at the time of her death had opportunity in the previous years to infect any of her male partners. The accusation of contamination will recur again but for now the police had a full list of previous acquaintances that they were eager to question. Either to eliminate them, or to see if any of them matched the description given by Robert Roberts.

Inspector Neil had a full list: -

Suspects - various

Bert Melvin, George Wright, Thomas Atkins, William Lineham, William Russell, Henry Biddle, William Herbert Tetlow, J Hurst (known as 'Jumbo') Jack Carr, and Frank Maidment.

The man Bert Melvin was found to be William Melvin, a glass and scientific instrument maker of 52 Clerkenwell Rd. He was single, fond of drink and loose women. Although living in Hendon with his parents, he volunteered to accompany Neil to Somers Town Police Station, where he was seen by Robert Roberts, Frank Clarke, Edward Smyth and others. All of whom stated that he was well known at the 'Rising Sun', but had never been very familiar with Emily and was certainly not identical with the man seen in her company on the Monday night. On the night of 11th he had returned home early to Hendon.

George Wright was a conductor on a restaurant car of the Midland Railway travelling between London and Edinburgh. He left London on the 11.40am train, on 11th, and remained in Edinburgh on the night of the murder, returning to London at 11.15pm Thursday. His alibi was proven, but he had known Emily when she lived at Burton Crescent in 1905, and contracted venereal disease from her.

Thomas Atkins was a single man and up to about 18 months previous he had known Emily very well, but he had contracted venereal disease from her and was still suffering, being an out-patient at the Lock Hospital. On the evening of 11th he left off work at 6.30pm, and afterwards went to his lodgings at 42 Cumberland Market. He went to bed at 10pm and got up at 5.45am for work. This was borne out by his landlady and a fellow lodger. He also was seen by Roberts and the two prostitutes who stated he was not the man seen by them with deceased on the Monday.

William Lineham kept a brothel at 121 Judd St, where Emily had lived in 1906. During her time there, he had been charged and given 6 weeks Hard Labour for running a brothel. He appeared to blame Emily for this, and was said to have borne her a grudge.

On the night of the murder, he was at home the whole of the evening with his wife at 46 Union St, Talmouth Road, Borough. This was confirmed by his landlady Mrs Evans, and Roberts and the other witnesses also stated that he was not the man they had seen at the 'Rising Sun'.

Robert Roberts was still being retained as a helper for the police and paid by the Police Informant Fund to identify the mystery man at the 'Rising Sun'. Many people were able to describe him but no one knew his name.

The search continued.

William Russell was an Army Reserve man living with a prostitute known as Scotch Barbara, at 20 Cummings St, Pentonville. He was living off the immoral earnings of Scotch Barbara, whose correct name was Barbara Thompson.

None of the witnesses recognised him as Emily's male friend.

Henry Biddle, who has been mentioned before, was a yeoman of signals serving on HMS Prince of Wales attached to the Mediterranean fleet. The ship was at Malta at the time of the murder with Biddle aboard. However, he had told his friends that he too had contracted venereal disease from Emily, and as a result they had quarrelled and parted. He set sail and Emily returned to her old ways in London.

Wiliam Herbert Tetlow was found to be a married man living at 163 High Holborn, employed by a firm of woollen merchants in Golden Square. He denied having any relationship with Emily and his account was believed.

'Jumbo' Hurst has already been accounted for.

Jack Carr's name was mentioned by deceased's sister Mrs Coleman. He knew Emily when she was employed as a servant in East Finchley.

Neil's enquiries showed that Jack Carr was living in Belfast, having moved there from Glasgow. He entered into enquiries as possibly being the man 'Scotch Bob', that was known to be an associate of Emily of whom she was said to be afraid. However, Jack Carr hadn't been in London for at least two years.

Frank Maidment was a fellow worker of George Wright already mentioned above and knew Emily when at Burton Crescent. Like Wright, Maidment was in Edinburgh at the time of the murder.

Neil was contacted by a Mrs Atkins to enquire after a Albert Arnold. He was living in Finsbury Park. He, like the others, was fond of prostitutes and had been a patient at the Lock hospital. However, he denied any knowledge of Emily, and did not fit the description of Roberts, and was dropped from enquiries.

Suspect No 5 — John Crabtree

Neil then turned to one of Emily's former landlords, the habitual recidivist John William Crabtree. He was currently serving a sentence of four months hard labour in Pentonville Prison for keeping a brothel.

Crabtree had no hesitation in recalling a man who had practically lived with Emily during her time at 1, Bidborough Street. The man had a violent temper and had been known to threaten Emily, and at one time assaulted her. The man Crabtree described fitted the description given by Roberts and others at the 'Rising Sun'.

The name of the man in the blue serge suit was unknown to Crabtree, who nevertheless was convinced that he was responsible for Emily's death. His wife had also seen the man around and about the Kings Cross area since her husband had been in prison. Neil's search continued. He concluded his report on 30 September by saying: 'I and my officers are of the opinion that the murderer will not be traced until this man is found and every possible effort is being made with that object in view.'

One name that kept recurring during these early days was that of 'Scotch Bob'. No one knew who this person was or even his real name. May Campbell referred to him as well, but only on information given to her from Roberts. His identity remained as elusive as the prime suspect. 'Scotch Bob' was said to be known as Bob Machonockie, Robert Bruce or Robert Burn, and to be frequenter of race meetings. Jack Carr was also thought to be 'Scotch Bob'.

Crabtree was later to state that many men, amongst them 'Scotch Bob' had threatened Emily with harm.

He called one 'Scotty', a motor driver. I like to think that this was some form of dark humour on the part of Crabtree in naming Carr a driver. Whatever the truth 'Scotch Bob' failed to materialise.

Robert MacCowan — witness for the prosecution

Whilst efforts were made to locate the male friend of Emily and also 'Scotch Bob', at one time considered to be the same person, another line of enquiry opened.

Dr Thompson the Divisional Surgeon had confirmed that death could have happened at any time between 3.00am and 5.00am, on the morning of September 12th. According to Inspector Neil, Robert Henry MacCowan came forward voluntarily to state that he had seen a man leave 29 St Pauls Road, at about 4.45am, on the morning of the 12th. Some reports have him marked as a police informer but there is little to confirm this.

He made his statement on the 14th September adding that he was an unemployed carman on the railway, and was looking for work in Brewery Road which is a through road to Kings Cross sidings. A little further up is Market Street, a wide road down which the cattle were driven from off the goods trains and to the abbatoir. In the early 1950s when I went to Hungerford School, the smell of slaughter was always in the air.

Ruby Young, as sketched by Robert Wood.

MacCowan lived in Hawley Street, Kentish Town. There are various ways of walking to Kings Cross but most lead across Kentish Town and Camden Road and into St Pauls Road.

His testimony in court was ripped apart by Marshall Hall, as MacCowan claimed to have seen the man leave clearly by the glow of the street light. It was established that the lights had already been extinguished, and his evidence was made unsafe. However, at the time he first made his statement he was adamant that although he did not see the man's face clearly, he would be able to recognise him again by the peculiarity in his walk.

The 'Rising Sun' postcard

Then Neil was blessed with more good fortune. Bert Shaw had decided to move out of 29 St Pauls Road, and on 25th September, when clearing out a chest of drawers found the 'Rising Sun' postcard between the lining of newspapers.

Most of Emily's collection were in albums that had been scattered around the living room. This one had been secreted where no one might look. Certainly not the killer if it was postcards and evidence of his relationship that he was searching for.

This postcard and three others from the collection were found to be in the same handwriting, and presumably from the same sender as the charred letter. On the authority of Sir Melville MacNaughton,

Assistant Commissioner, the 'Rising Sun' postcard and the others were handed to the press for publication.

These appeared in the daily papers on the 28th and 29th of September. There was no response to this until on October 4th, after the photograph was published in the *News of the World* on Sunday 29th September. Ruby Young, described as an Artists Model but really a high class prostitute, of 2, Finborough Road, Earls Court, had some information.

Suspect No 6 - Robert Wood

Ruby Young recognised the handwriting.

It was that of Robert William George Cavers Wood. She had known him for almost two years, when she was living close to the Angel, Islington. Their relationship had ended earlier in 1907, and she had seen little of him since.

Then out of the blue he had asked to meet her again, and on agreeing Ruby was asked by Wood to provide an alibi for him, by saying that they always met each other on Mondays and Wednesdays. She had agreed thinking that it was no more than a little white lie to protect his father from knowing his real interest in the back streets of Kings Cross.

On the 29th September the postcard was published. Emily's photograph had already appeared in the press, and forced into a corner Wood admitted that he had written the postcard but had not wanted to enter into a formal arrangement with Emily. He continued to press the accidental nature of his meetings with Emily, and for Ruby to account for his movements on the evening of September 11th, even to the point of detailing each show and bar they had visited.

In the end Ruby could not carry on the deception any further. Wood continued to make excuses for not informing the police and Ruby contacted them herself.

Her next actions were to bring unjustified disgrace and public humiliation pouring down on her. On that evening of 4th October, Neil accompanied Ruby to the Grays Inn Road at 6.15pm when Wood finished work. She identified Wood to Inspector Neil and from that moment her name was 'Judas'.

Neil conveyed Wood to Highgate Police Station and took his statement. In it Wood admitted the following:

(1) that he first made the acquaintance of Emily Dimmock in a casual way on the Friday preceding the murder.

(2) that he consented to send her a card and wrote on it at her request 'Phyllis darling if it pleases you meet me at 8.15pm at the – sketch of a rising sun – Yours to a cinder Alice.'

He signed it 'Alice' she saying that he better send it that way in case her 'old man' should see it.

He stated that although he wrote the card he had no intention of keeping the appointment.

(3) That he did not write the letter making an appointment for the night of the murder.

(4) That he was in the company of Miss Ruby Young aforementioned on the evening of the murder, leaving her about 11.pm and proceeding to his own house which he reached about midnight.

(5) That he admits being in the company of the deceased woman at the time of the appointment.

Statements (4) and (5) appear contradictory unless Wood is referring to the Monday at the 'Rising Sun'.

Neil remarked that the handwriting on the postcard and on the charred remains of the letter appeared to be that of Robert Wood and that the statement regarding Ruby Young was false.

Neil's next task was to arrange an identification parade. Wood was placed amongst 15 other men. Roberts and his friend Frank Clarke had no hesitation in identifying Robert Wood as the man they had seen in Emily's company on Monday, September 9th.

The next person to attend was John Crabtree. He was sure he was going to be asked to identify the man he knew as 'Scotch Bob', and whom he was convinced had committed the offence.

When unable to pick out Wood he said to Neil: 'There is a man here that I know but he's not the man I have been speaking about; but there is a man there that knows Phyllis Dimmock.'

He refused to touch the man, re-iterated that he was

not the man he referred to but finally identified him, and touched Wood but refused to make a statement.

All Crabtree would do was to state that he was aware that Wood had been an acquaintance of Emily for a long time and from that Neil understood that Wood had been a frequent visitor of Emily's whilst she was staying at 1, Bidborough Street and 13, Manchester Street.

Having established the link he was looking for Neil charged Robert Wood with the wilful murder of Emily Elizabeth Dimmock.

On Sunday 6th, Wood was again placed up for identification at various times. He was identified by Ellen Lawrence, who had known him as an acquaintance of the deceased for about eighteen months. She had seen them together on the Friday and Monday evenings prior to the murder. Emily Stewart (aka Florence Smith) and Edward Charles Smith identified him as being in the company of the deceased on Friday and Monday night.

William and Gladys Lineham with whom Emily had lodged identified Wood as an acquaintance of hers of about eighteen months standing. Albert Miller, the window cleaner also identified Wood as the man he had seen arguing with the soldier 'Jumbo' Hurst.

Emily Crabtree, wife of John Crabtree, was also given an opportunity of identifying Wood from amongst the others. She was asked in the usual way to touch anyone amongst those present whom she knew. Amongst those present was a dark, clean shaven young man similar in appearance to Robert Wood. He stood No 1 on the line, Wood standing No 2. She touched No1 and was then asked to stand to one side. Being under the impression that a mistake had been made by her and not having any reason to keep the men who had all been called in from the adjoining thoroughfare, No 1 was allowed to leave with the others.

After he had gone Mrs Crabtree said to Neil: 'You know there were two men there who knew Phyllis Dimmock. I knew they both used to visit her. The one I touched first and the one who stood next to him. I suppose I ought to have touched them both.'

I suppose we will never know who No 1 was. It was not 'Scotch Bob' or she would have spotted him at once. The formal dress of white collar workers was a blue serge suit and bowler hat. It would have been a simple task to go out into the street and find 14 other young men in their mid twenties dressed similarly. The chances of finding one other man who knew the victim were obviously high but this was Edwardian London and the double life led by Robert Wood was quite common. Many young men of undoubted character on the outside were well known to frequent the bars and houses that the Crabtrees knew well.

All that Neil could do was to take a statement from her in which she says that Wood visited the deceased once in 1, Bidborough Street in June 1906, and about three times in 13 Manchester Street afterwards.

At 9.10am on Monday 7th October, Wood was placed with 11 other men and they were requested to walk round the yard. This was for the benefit of the unemployed carman Robert MacCowan, who was able to identify Wood as the man he had seen leave 29 St Pauls Road, by the nature of his walk.

Wood appeared at Clerkenwell Police Court before the presiding Magistrate on the same day and was remanded in custody until Tuesday 15th.

On 8th October, Joseph Lambert visited Kentish Town Police Station.

It will be recalled that Lambert was a friend of Wood, and had stopped for a drink with him in the 'Eagle' on September 11th. He confirmed that meeting, saying that he arrived about 8.45pm. He stayed for no longer than fifteen minutes during which time he spoke to both Wood and Emily who apologised for her appearance. She said that she had only popped out of the house to post a letter.

This was true. She was going to post a card to her sister Maud at Putney. The post card was duly posted, bears the Camden Town postmark and time 9.45pm, and was received by her sister the following morning.

Whether Emily really did just pop out to post a letter or used it as an excuse to meet her appointment is unknown. She made no effort to make herself presentable, very much in the style of anyone who rushes out of the house to complete a menial task.

When Lambert left, Emily and Wood were still together.

On 13th September, the morning newspapers were full with details of Emily's murder. Robert Wood must have known that he would be the prime suspect and began to prepare his alibi. He rang Joseph Lambert but the latter did not want to discuss such things on the phone, and they agreed to meet later that evening.

Robert Wood told Lambert that he could mention that they had met for a drink on the Wednesday evening, but asked him to leave the girl out of it. This conversation must have rung alarm bells in Lambert's head, and following the publication of the 'Rising Sun' postcard with Wood's handwriting easily identifiable, he had no choice but to clear himself from any involvement in the crime.

Inspector Neil was now certain that he had the murderer and Wood was sent for trial at the Old Bailey. The evidence against him was not completely watertight. Neil was certain that Wood had known Emily for a long time - maybe two years or more. He was the last person to be seen in her company and a man fitting his description was seen leaving the scene of the crime shortly after death was said to have occurred.

The alibi that Wood had tried to secure for himself

was now exposed as a lie. He had lied about his relationship with Emily, and had tried to get other people such as Lambert to lie for him as well. Ruby Young had been drawn into the plot, and she too had been asked to provide false witness statements.

When Arthur Newton presented the papers to Marshall Hall, the latter knew immediately that he had a fight on his hands. He turned to his junior Wellesley Orr with this remark: 'I want you to concentrate on this case entirely for the next three weeks. This is the greatest case I've ever had in my life. If you have an idea, however remote or far-fetched, come in and tell me. The man's innocent, and a chance idea may mean life or death to him.'

4 THE TRIAL OF ROBERT WOOD

The Camden Town Murder as it quickly became known, occurred in a poor quarter of North London. The victim, her common law husband, her close friends and acquaintances were unashamedly working class, and many flirted with the underworld.

Yet, within a few months, the rich and famous, professionals and men of high rank, were set against one another in a court case that transfixed the nation, and made it one of the greatest ever contested.

It is worth stepping back a moment from the actual crime, to take stock of those that gathered in the Old Bailey courtroom, to decide on the fate of a man who was but a step away from the gallows.

The many players and bit part actors would have graced any West End performance. At the centre of which was the stage itself – the Old Bailey, or to give it its correct title, the Central Criminal Court.

The Old Bailey, now a world wide institution, was built on the site of the old Newgate prison. For centuries Newgate Hill and the area around was the scene of floggings and mutilations, heretics and others were burned at the stake, and it was of course a popular place for public hangings. In 1834, the Old Bailey, which was a building erected to hear criminal cases before sentencing and conveying to Newgate Prison itself, was established as the principal court for London and the South East circuit.

In 1902, Newgate Prison was itself demolished to make way for the current building which was opened in 1907 by Edward VII. Charles Mathews QC who was to appear for the crown against Robert Wood was knighted at a special ceremony on its opening.

Arthur John Newton

It was of some poignancy to Robert Wood himself. He wrote to his brother Charles after the first day of the trial; 'Little did I think that one day I should appear on the capital charge, under that beautiful figure of Justice (by Frampton RA) that towers above the Old Bailey. I think you have admired it. I have a memory of sitting with this great sculptor on more than one occasion. I am rather cut off now from Mr Newton….'

He was referring to Arthur John Newton, his

solicitor. But of some small interest is that Wood signed himself 'Bob'. It is a familiar shortening of Robert, but if he had used this term with those close to him it is no wonder that he was so often thought of as being the mysterious 'Scotch Bob'. He had moved down from Edinburgh with his father although no one appears to have made any remarks as to the strength or peculiarity of any accent.

Newton's association with Marshall Hall had begun in 1894, when he had instructed Hall in a case involving an Austrian prostitute named Marie Hermann, who stood accused of murdering an old gentleman with a poker.

Newton would normally have taken the case to a more prominent barrister as there had been great public interest shown, but the fee was minimal, only ten guineas, and Marshall Hall was still looking to make a name. He had not yet handled a big case and he took this opportunity with both hands.

Marie Hermann was acquitted. Hall had argued for self-defence and had persuaded the judge and jury accordingly. At the conclusion of the trial Marie Hermann instructed her attorney to ask for an account of how the fees were made up, as she had contributed towards them. Newton's reply was terse and to the point: 'Dear Sir, we saved your client from the gallows.'

Newton continued to bring quality cases to Marshall Hall whose reputation was growing. Much earlier in

1889, having just set up his own practice in Grafton Street, Tottenham Court Road, he had been involved in the Cleveland Street Scandal. This had involved many so-called respectable members of the upper classes and titled ranks, being discovered as regular clients at a brothel in Cleveland Street, also just off Tottenham Court Road. This was opposite the studios of Walter Sickert and one of the high profile clients was none other than the Duke of Clarence, the future King of England. Both suspected of being Jack the Ripper.

Newton was to be instrumental in Wood's defence but even he had little faith in his client. On the evening before the trial began, he wrote this to Hall: 'I spent an enormous time with Wood. We cannot call him. You were perfectly right in every way.'

This was in response to Hall's own assessment of Wood: 'I can't call him. He's raving mad. Wood's raving mad.'

Judge William Grantham

Whether or not this was the truth, it was not for Marshall Hall or Newton to decide. If the matter of Wood's sanity was to be discussed, it would have been at the behest of the presiding judge, William Grantham.

He was born in October 1835, educated at Kings College School, London and called to the Bar in January 1863. The Dictionary of National Biography

Judge William Grantham

was none too kind: he obtained the reputation of being *'a very useful junior in an action on a builder's account, in a running-down case, in a compensation case, and especially in disputes in which a combined knowledge of law and horseflesh was desirable.'*

He had a habit of talking too much in trials over which he was presiding and interrupting both counsel. His peers did not consider this the way for a judge to behave, and towards the close of his career he was given strong hints in the press that the public interest would be best served by his retirement.

Grantham's summing-up at the end of Wood's trial was considered controversial at the time and many modern commentators have tried to explain it, usually unsatisfactorily. He consistently came to verbal blows with Marshall Hall during the trial, something which had been very noticeable whenever their professional paths had crossed.

Few of the major players were strangers to each other. Marshall Hall had been opposing counsel to Charles Mathews on many occasions. They were used to each others strengths as well as weaknesses, and they were in court to act out the play once more.

Charles Mathews, usually known as 'Willie' Mathews was the son of an actress and he employed many of the actors effects in court. He had a slightly feminine face and a high pitched voice but one which was

Edward Marshall Hall

impossible to ignore. His style could best be described as histrionic but very effective in persuading a jury.

Edward Marshall Hall QC

The man who had most to gain and possibly most to lose after the accused was Marshall Hall himself. In 1907 his career was in decline.

He was born in Old Steyne, Brighton, in September 1858. His father was a physician, but Edward followed his grandfather's path and became a solicitor and then a barrister. His early years were spent devilling for many of the leading lights and he soon got a reputation for his brilliant advocacy in court.

One of the first 'causes celèbres' was that mentioned above – many more followed and his star was in the ascendant. Then in 1900, he defended an actress who was at the centre of a libel case involving the *Daily Mail.* They impugned that she was the mother of another music hall star whose age was actually only a couple of years younger. This was obviously an error and the paper published an apology.

However it was not considered enough for the actress, claiming the apology made matters worse. The *Mail* asked for time to investigate but after three weeks no further action had been taken.

Marshall Hall claimed for damages which were granted at £1000. He then exacerbated the matter by restating that the apology aggravated the libel, and that they had spent three weeks trying to find out more stories about the actress without success. Further he added; ' My client may have to work for her living but her reputation is entitled to the same consideration as any in the land, including Mrs Alfred Harmsworth (her husband being the owner of the *Daily Mail*.)'.

As a consequence the jury increased the damages to £2500.

This angered Harmsworth. He immediately launched an appeal, which was upheld by the Law Lords at the Court of Appeal, and Marshall Hall was severely censured for implying that the *Daily Mail* had tried for three more weeks to seek out any information whatsoever to further blacken the actress' name.

Hall's reputation was dragged through the press – not just in Harmsworth's papers but in every national title. The censure of the Law Lords and the Court of Appeal was a heavy crime. Harmsworth also took offence at the perceived slight against his wife.

Marshall Hall's caseload and therefore his income slumped. Few cases came his way – those that did were poorly paid.

Then in 1905, after accepting good advice from a friend, Marshall Hall apologised to Harmsworth. The latter accepted it and slowly Hall's name appeared more favourably in the pages devoted to legal matters.

But it would be a long way back before he would

reach the heights that he had achieved by the turn of the century.

Thus it was a stroke of good fortune that Newton came into his chambers with the papers on Robert Wood and the murder of Emily Dimmock.

The Court

On 12th December 1907, when the court convened, the class divide that was England was arraigned in court.

The social and economic background of Edwardian England provides a valuable backdrop to this case. The following provide some clues as to the kind of life endured by the ordinary person around the beginning of the century.

This is a letter from a reader of the *Radio Times* writing in 1971:

"'I read Benny Green's article on Tommy Steele's TV presentation (*Radio Times*, 8 April). I am in my 74th year and have no television, and I do not know who Benny Green is. But I suspect he knows little about the Edwardian era or Music Hall. True there was poverty (I knew plenty of it), bad sanitation, and what have you. That is why we went to the theatre and the Music Hall, to escape from everyday life. We really enjoyed ourselves wholeheartedly, unlike most of the modern generation who seem to take everything far too seriously, even their pleasures. But when Benny Green describes that decade as 'a great hypocritical fraud, a confidence trick and a disgrace to civilisation', he makes me hot under the collar. Of course the Edwardian working classes could sing happy, boisterous songs - and they did with gusto. To describe it as spurious shows how little Mr Green knows about it. I am willing to stick my neck out and say, along with thousands of my own age group, 'Thank God I was alive in the much-maligned Edwardian era'."

This was the age of the music hall and the public house. Drink was the easiest and most accessible way to escape, even if only for a few hours the poverty, gloomy streets and squalid housing. Each adult was thought to consume at last three pints of beer a day.

Sex was taboo and nakedness forbidden, although oral historical research shows that morals were rather more free and easy in some working class circles, and among country folk.

There were two distinct worlds; one of chastity and family life; and the other pleasure and the gratification of desires. The result was a separate set of morals for each sex. A woman was expected to adhere to a code of rigorous purity, and utter contempt was meted out to the girl who had been seduced, and become a 'fallen woman'. A man, on the other hand, was perfectly free to combine a happy family life, with the pursuit of outside pleasures in the company of women from a different social class.

On one side the law; Justice Grantham – a model of an English country gentleman and founder of the Pegasus Club devoted to those who appreciate a fine horse – Charles Mathews – recently knighted when the Old Bailey was re-opened – and Marshall Hall – perhaps England's finest criminal defence barrister.

Watching the proceedings was the jury. Anyone appearing on the electoral roll is now eligible for jury duty. There are some exceptions, but generally if you are of sound mind, not serving in the military or a prison sentence and are between 18 and 65, then it is unlikely that you will pass through adult life without being called up for jury service.

Not so in 1907. Jurors were from a very narrow section of the community. Qualification was dependent on property ownership, and restricted to men between the ages of 21 and 70. The Jury lists drawn up to meet these specifications were then arranged alphabetically in groups of 25, so that there was a strict rotation of jurors called to serve.

Qualification also relied upon property ownership and there had to be proof of residency for at least 16 months. In addition, only the head of the household was eligible for jury service so that only about three out of five adults ever appeared.

As qualification was based on residency there were few jurors selected from the working classes. Many of them were in debt, a large proportion permanently in transit, moving from one rented accommodation to another to escape debt. One is reminded of the famous music hall song - 'My old man said follow the van'. These lower classes dreaded any registration as that meant they might be traced. The composition of juries was very middle-class.[1]

A contemporary photograph shows the jury that was summoned to hear the case against Robert Wood. All the men appear solidly middle class, soberly dressed and listening with a dignified and attentive manner. The trial hinged on the history of sexual relations between a respectable artist and what Inspector Neil called the 'demi-monde'; who knows what could have passed through the minds of those twelve good men and true.

Across from the jury and sitting in the public gallery by applying for a limited number of tickets were London's literati and artistic alumni – H B Irving, A E W Mason, Sir George Alexander, Sir Arthur Pinero, Oscar Asche, and Seymour Hicks amongst others.

Waiting outside to be called into the witness box were a collection of prostitutes, pimps, brothel-keepers, thieves, the unemployed and working men standing on the brink of starvation, and the steps leading down into the criminal underclasses.

In the middle, his life in the balance was Robert Wood. He was an educated man, artistically gifted living in some comfort with a good salary. Yet, a man who had worked and dined with some of the men in the public gallery, those that had come to watch the battle for his life, had a foot in both camps.

This was the paradox that was Robert Wood. A few years later in the trial of Edward Lawrence in 1908, Marshall Hall first introduced what was to become his trademark – a speech containing the dramatic illustration of the 'Scales of Justice'.

His hands became the hands of the scales over the Old Bailey building that had so captivated Robert Wood. The scales tipped this way, then the other. It was so closely a comment on Robert Wood who lived by day as a sober, respected draughtsman, and by night inhabited the underworld of London's Kings Cross and the lives of its people. Both sides of the court were in the balance and the scales were tipped dramatically up and down as the weight of evidence was proven and dismissed.

One person continued to beaver away – Arthur Newton. He had been retained by Wood's company, the Sand and Blast Manufacturing Company Limited, who obviously had great faith in their employee and stood by him to such an extent as to employ the services of one of London's top solicitors.

On the eve of the trial Newton wrote to Hall expressing his doubts as to the wisdom of putting Wood in the witness box. He concluded his letter by adding: 'I have a most important piece of information which I think may turn the course of events.'

That information was vital to Marshall Hall and he used it to great effect on the final day. Of some further small interest is the reliance on the post. There is little faith these days in the ability of the postal services to delivery a first class letter by the next morning. At the turn of the century, letters posted the previous evening thudded on to hallways first thing next morning. The speed of the postal service was yet another weapon in Marshall Hall's armoury.

The case for the Prosecution

On the morning of December 12th 1907, the case opened. The first of 35 witnesses for the prosecution was then called.

Much of Marshall Hall's life and work has been carefully annotated by his biographer Edward Marjoribanks. For the most part, the author has the utmost respect for his subject, though on occasions bordering on idolatry. There is little criticism, and even in the libel case mentioned above many pages are spent defending Marshall Hall's decision. However,

Marjoribanks account of the trials have become the standard work for all future commentators including Sir David Napley in his own book on this case.

Large chunks of Marjoribanks work continue to appear in magazines and books. In the absence of the actual case transcripts, I will go along with his version of the trial like everybody else. Rather than quote from every witness, I will concentrate on the evidence given by the principal characters, as this will eventually help to explain my own conclusions.

Among the first witnesses called were Emily's brother Henry who had been asked to identify her body. Bert Shaw was called, and for a moment it appeared as if Marshall Hall was trying to dislodge an alibi that had been proven to be watertight. Another witness was the Police Surgeon Dr Thompson who was able to testify as to time of death.

The star turn of the first day was the ship's cook Robert Roberts. Marshall Hall first got him to admit that he knew the woman May Campbell, who had gone to the police to give him an alibi. Then, the matter of the letter found in the grate was discussed. Roberts continued to hold to his story that it read: 'Dear Phyllis, will you meet me at the 'Eagle' tonight, Bert'.

There were two matters that concerned Marshall Hall. First he expressed his doubts as to the actual existence of a letter having been posted at all, possibly implying that Roberts had written it himself. For, he asked, why would someone arrange for an appointment for 'tonight' when the letter appeared to have been posted on the previous Tuesday evening, for it to arrive first thing Wednesday morning. He would have meant Tuesday night.

Secondly, why did the writer sign themselves 'Bert'. Was this to throw suspicion on Bert Shaw? But Robert Roberts could equally have been a Bert and as above Robert Wood had signed himself 'Bob'.

This was a strange line of enquiry from Hall. The handwriting on the letter had been proven to have come from the same person as the postcard, and Neil had more than once referred to the style of writing as one from an educated man. Roberts was not that, but he knew that after Wood he was next in line to be accused, so that he had tried anything to shift the blame. Perhaps Hall was doing no more than placing doubt in the jury's mind.

The second day saw Roberts' friend Frank Clarke in the witness box, who was as confused as Judge Grantham by Halls' question, as to whether Roberts had spent the three nights with Emily – on the Monday, Tuesday and Sunday. By admitting to the 'three nights' Clarke had implied that Roberts had spent Wednesday night with Emily, which he hadn't. Judge Grantham asked Hall to express himself better but it left the court confused. However, their landlady had testified that both men had returned to their rooms on the night of Wednesday 11th September.

The final witness on the second day was the unemployed carman Robert MacCowan. His benefit to the prosecution had already been diminished, when at previous committal hearings Newton had questioned him over his ability to be able to recognise the man leaving 29 St Pauls Road, by the street light. The lights had already been extinguished at the time he originally stated, and his revised statement giving a much earlier time was therefore doubtful.

He had later to admit that he had mentioned No 29, after he had read it in the papers. He then mentioned it had been a 'drizzly, foggy morning'. It had in fact been very fine – September had been one of the warmest for years.

Slowly, his testimony was being destroyed by Hall. Then he mentioned that the man had a peculiar walk. This led to witnesses being called who confirmed that Wood did have a strange walk, but as Hall pointed out, he could call as many witnesses as the prosecution to admit that there was nothing odd about Wood's walk at all.

Many of the witnesses had been to identity parades and spotted Wood by his walk, including MacCowan, but he had proved a bad witness. His story was later given credence by Ruby Young, but the man left court to a bitter outburst from the crowd who accused him of being a police informer.

I can find no trace of him being paid out of the Police Informant Fund; Roberts was the main recipient owing to his first hand knowledge of Wood. MacCowan appears to have come forward in the genuine belief that he was helping the police. I doubt if he would have done so again!

The third day was highlighted by the testimony of Ruby Young. She was the one to have recognised his handwriting on the 'Rising Sun' postcard. She was the one to point him out in Grays Inn Road to Inspector Neil and then she made a most telling statement that Robert Wood had a 'peculiarity in his walk that no one could copy'. It gave credence to MacCowan's testimony. She also mentioned his way of holding his right hand in his pocket to disguise a childhood injury, that accentuated his way of walking.

Then came the false alibi that Wood had asked her to give him. It appeared damning.

It was not to be. It was perhaps Marshall Hall's greatest moment in the trial. He put this question to Ruby, but no doubt looking at the jury all the time: 'Having regard to Doctor Thompson's evidence that the deceased woman was murdered between three and four in the morning, has it ever struck you that this was a perfectly useless alibi for the murderer, but a perfect alibi for a meeting with the girl?'

Ruby answered; 'No'.

As has been said, Robert Wood came from a respectable family and even his employers had little idea of his nocturnal habits. It was Marshall Hall's contention that Wood asked Ruby Young for an alibi solely to protect his reputation; and to protect his father who was a very sick man, from the public humiliation it would bring, if the police were to arrest him. It was an alibi concocted by a man who had no idea of the time of murder, but needed to distance himself from the victim who was well known as a prostitute.

Poor Ruby Young never recovered from this. However gentle Hall had been with her in the witness box the public spared her no sympathy. She was called 'Judas' and on the final day had to be smuggled out of the court in the clothes of a charlady. The mob shouted out after her : 'Ruby, Ruby – won't you come out tonight.' Public sympathy was already with Robert Wood and no doubt the solid citizens in the jury were experiencing similar feelings.

The next day, Mathews called many of the women who usually paraded along the Euston Road, all of whom were able to testify that Emily had known Robert Wood for longer than the six days that he admitted.

The final witness to be called for the prosecution was the rogue John William Crabtree. He, like many of

Charles Mathews QC

Emily's female acquaintances testified that she had known Wood for many years, and he had seen her in company with him.

Unfortunately for Crabtree he had to face Marshall Hall. First, he had to admit that in his case, 'no fixed abode' meant that he was currently serving a term of hard labour for running a brothel. Secondly, he recounted his previous convictions amongst which was one for horse-stealing, guaranteed to put him out of favour with the pedigree horse expert, Judge Grantham.

Having had his character blackened, Crabtree then proved an asset to Hall, by claiming that when he went to the identification parade he had expected to see 'Scotch Bob', not Robert Wood. This 'Scotty' was the man Crabtree expected to turn out to be the murderer. He was a motor driver. Crabtree then recounted meeting this 'Scotty', who had threatened Emily with a knife. But then so had the sailor Henry Biddle.

On the whole, Crabtree did not make a good witness which must have pleased Hall, for the next day the defence began in earnest.

The case for the Defence

In his own inimitable style, and in keeping with the tenor of the trial he found fault with the way the case had been handled – a slight on the judge himself. Hall questioned, as to why evidence from two men by the names of Sharples and Harvey, had not been called into court by the prosecution. If a man such as Crabtree can be called why not those two.

Those two were well known pimps in the Kings Cross area, who had approached the police stating that at about 12.30am on the morning of 12th September, they had seen Emily Dimmock in the company of another, larger man who did not fit the description of the accused.

Apparently it was such a rousing speech the courtroom burst into applause. The two men were not called although within the law their statement was read out in court. Inspector Neil had already dismissed this evidence. Emily was a popular figure, often seen in the bars and eating houses, and if it was Emily that Sharples and Harvey saw, why had no one else seen her?

It was time to call his first witness which was Wood's father. The latter recalled Robert coming home at about midnight on the 11th of September. Asked how he remembered this, George Wood explained how a bottle of skin lotion had been spilled which had been remarked upon by his son.

This was corroborated by Wood's half-brother George, and verified by a tenant in the flat above the Woods'. This man was an avid angler, and at about ten minutes to midnight was out in the garden digging for worms when he saw Robert Wood come home.

111

The next witness explained the important news about which Newton had written to Hall on the evening preceding the opening day. Hall called William Westcott. He was a ticket collector on the Midland Railway who usually left for work at about 4.30am. He was also an amateur boxer and part of his training regime included his walk to work. It gave him a certain style to his walk, which Hall suggested was the man that MacCowan had seen in St Pauls Road.

Having established that Wood had arrived home at midnight and had been mistaken for another man, at the time that the murderer could have been escaping from the scene of his crime, Marshall Hall ceded to the advice of his junior Wellesley Orr and called Robert Wood into the witness box.

This was a bold move. The passing of the Criminal Evidence Act of 1898 gave prisoners the right to give evidence in their own defence. It was not universally welcomed, as many advocates saw this as a two edged sword, where skilful cross examination by the prosecution counsel could lead to defendants failing to give a good account of themselves and paying with their life as a result.

This was not lost on Marshall Hall for although the Act was seen as a mark of progress, up until this trial no prisoner called to give evidence in his own defence on a capital charge had escaped the gallows. It was a rule of practice that the defendant be the first to give evidence. It was not the law, and in this instance Marshall Hall called Robert Wood last.

Wood was not a good witness. He was loved by his friends but this was sometimes expressed as vanity and many considered him a poseur. Marshall Hall aimed for the most dramatic opening; 'Robert Wood, did you kill Emily Dimmock?'

Robert Wood remained silent.

By now the effect was lost, but Hall persevered. 'You must answer straight.'

'I mean it is ridiculous' Wood finally replied.

None of his following testimony would have endeared him to jury still sitting with an open mind. He denied knowing Crabtree, he claimed he could never be seen in public with a girl wearing hair curlers, as Emily was on the night of 11th September in the 'Eagle'; and finally, he denied going into public houses, especially the 'Rising Sun' which he knew had a poor reputation.

In his final piece of testimony, he failed to admit to having written the charred letter found in the grate, expressing an opinion that it was a copy. Having been given a chance to explain the reason for the letter or its contents, he threw it away.

On the sixth and final day, he was cross examined by Charles Mathews. He denied being engaged to Ruby Young, despite having given her a ring: 'It was something pleasing to her,' he said. At no time would he give a straightforward answer. In an earlier cross examination, Hall had insisted to Grantham that he had never implied that Wood had a sexual relationship with Emily. Asked if he had been in Emily's rooms on the night of 11th September, he again lost the opportunity for a straightforward denial: 'It is only to you Sir Charles, that I should answer that question. I should be indignant with the average man.'

For the final time, he was given a chance to explain the charred remains of the letter found in Emily's grate. Mathews had placed his own interpretation on the few words or part words that were still decipherable:

'Will you .... ar ...of the ...miss ..Town ... S
...ill... Wednesday ... has ... and ... rest ...
excuse ... good ... fond ... Mon ... from '

Which Mathews interpreted as: 'Will you meet me at the bar of the 'Eagle' near Camden Town Station on Wednesday 8.15. ... goodbye ... fondest love .. from'

This was close to Roberts remembrance of the letter but Wood still resisted any opportunity to offer his own version. 'I cannot make head or tail of it.'

He admitted meeting Emily on the Monday evening in the 'Rising Sun' which was the invitation on the postcard, but denied making any other assignation. Mathews suggested that having made one appointment by post he had since made another. Wood denied it.

His ordeal was over but he had made a bad impression on most people in court.

The Verdict

Robert Wood had remained a dispassionate observer throughout the trial. Many in the court were shocked to learn that he had spent his time in the dock sketching many of the court officials, including Judge Grantham, which he completed whilst his subject was summing up.

It was strange behaviour. From the outset, Marshall Hall and Newton had been reluctant to call him to the witness box. Their fears had been confirmed, but there was nothing more now that Hall could do but plead for his life for a final time to the jury.

The rules governing the order of final speeches has changed since 1907. The last person to address the jury would necessarily have the greatest impact on them, but as evidence had been called by the defence, Marshall Hall was obliged to address the jury first. In 1964, the order of speeches was changed to allow the defence to have the final word. It was also customary for the accused to remain in the dock, whilst the jury deliberated rather than as today be returned to the cells to await their verdict.

The main plank of Hall's opening words was that this was a motiveless murder. No reason had been given for Robert Wood to have attacked Emily

Dimmock. Although he had lied about his movements on the night, and requested his former girlfriend Ruby Young and old friend Joseph Lambert to provide him with an alibi, his motives were borne out of a desire to save his family from the embarrassment of knowing about his double life.

Once again he tried to raise the question of the man seen with Emily by Sharples and Harvey. He was reprimanded once more by Judge Grantham, and concluded by reminding the jury of the evidence of the carman Robert MacCowan, and the late corroboration of Wood's peculiar style of walking by Ruby Young. Compared to his earlier treatment his final words were damning of her:

'The evidence of the carman stood alone in all its glaring improbability till December 4th, when two months after the arrest of her lover, Ruby Young for the first time said that he had a peculiar gait, similar to that described by the carman. That statement was invented out of revenge for the suggestion that her calling was the calling which in fact it was. So far as she was concerned it was a gross and vindictive lie. . . You cannot hang a man on evidence such as that. I defy you to do it. I defy you. I do not merely ask for a verdict of 'not guilty' – I demand it.'

Sir Charles Mathews rose to complete the prosecution case. He began by once again explaining Inspector Neil's reasons for not calling Sharples and Harvey, and then spoke of Robert Wood, calling him cold blooded. Certainly, there had been no show of emotion from the accused throughout the trial, and Mathews offered this as proof of his guilt.

There was no need to find a motive. That was how cold blooded killers behave; with no obvious reason for their behaviour. Mathews then countered Hall's remarks that no blood was found on Wood; simply because he had just left the deceased bed and there would have been no blood on his clothes because he wasn't wearing any. Similarly, there was no blood on his hands because he had wiped them clean in the wash basin, removing any last traces on Emily's petticoat.

By all accounts it was not one of Mathews best speeches. Perhaps, he had begun to have doubts himself. Nevertheless he continued to stress the cool, calm and collected manner of Wood who despite the almost daily appearance in the press of the murder maintained his sang froid throughout.

When Mathews sat down again, it was evident from the mood of the public gallery and of the crowds outside that their feelings were with Robert Wood. However, there was still the judge's summing up to come.

I was contacted by David Graham in New Zealand

(*above*) The jury
(*below*) A contemporary cartoon of
Charles Mathews QC

who is the great grandson of Judge Grantham. David Napley says in his account, that by no stretch of the imagination was Robert Wood fortunate in the choice of judge to preside over his trial. He referred to the unflattering comments in the Dictionary of National Biography, but might have made more impression on the reader, if he had been aware of David Graham's research that his great grandfather had sent 30 people to the gallows.

Judge Grantham began his summing up and slowly enumerated the case against Robert Wood:

'It must not be assumed that, because no motive has been shown on the part of the prisoner, therefore he must be "not guilty" … The whole evidence seems to prove that the prisoner has been leading a double life …There has been no explanation of the burnt letter, which is very strong indeed against the prisoner, and would justify the jury in believing the ship's cook's story … I think there is evidence to prove that the prisoner knew the murdered woman before September 6th …The evidence as to this showed that he was lying at the beginning, just as he lied at the end…. He says he is innocent yet he keeps everything from the police, and from his own brother.'

Then came the moment that astounded the court, and has ever since confounded commentators.

He continued: 'Although it is my duty to further the ends of justice, so that criminals are brought to justice and are properly convicted, however strongly circumstances may go against him, in my judgement, strong as the suspicion is, I do not think that the prosecution have brought the case home against him clearly enough.'

'Although it is a matter for you and for you alone, gentlemen, it is my duty to point out to you that, unless you find the evidence is so much against him as to warrant a conviction, you must give him the benefit of the doubt. I think gentlemen, I have spoke plainly to you. You are not bound to act on my view.'

Grantham concluded his summing up at 7.45pm, and the jury filed out to reach their decision leaving Wood in the dock to complete his sketch of Judge William Grantham.

At 8.00pm the jury returned and when asked for their verdict the foreman said loud and clear: 'Not Guilty'.

Both inside and outside the court, the crowds cheered. Robert Wood was whisked away to the Savoy Hotel in the Strand by Newton. Marshall Hall remained a while to receive the adulation. Poor Ruby Young was vilified.

It is difficult to understand why many writers have

found a problem with the judge's summing-up. Certainly, throughout the trial Grantham had been very critical of Robert Wood. It was plain from the outset that Wood had led a double life, and the veneer of respectability had soon been shattered. It is possible that his nocturnal existence was abhorrent to Grantham, and he saw before him a dissolute young man who had betrayed his class and brought shame on his family.

However, as a matter of law Grantham had no option but to direct the jury as he did. Wood had known Emily for some time and been seen in her company on the night of her death. Despite his lies and false alibis it was verified that he had returned home by midnight. This well before the time the murder took place, and whatever his reasons for constructing a false alibi, he was not found to have a motive for killing Emily and great doubts were cast on his being the man leaving 29 St Pauls Road, on 12th September.

The question therefore remains; if not Robert Wood, who did kill Emily Dimmock?

Notes

1. For this and other glimpses of Edwardian life I am grateful to my oldest friend Ron Marina, Head of History at Parmiters School, Watford.

5   'ROUND UP THE USUAL SUSPECTS'

At the conclusion of the trial, Inspector Neil wrote to his superiors: 'I venture to express the opinion that nothing further can be done in the matter …'

Anyone who has read the case file would have to admit that Neil did everything that was possible to try and uncover the culprit. Many men were interviewed, and one by one eliminated. Most of this has already been explained in Chapter Three.

Many years after the trial a play was written based on the Camden Town Murder by John van Druten called 'Somebody Knows.' I can find no copy of the play although it is frequently mentioned. It is an apt title – somebody must know but that somebody was either the murderer or someone who knew the identity but kept it quiet from the police and all other friends. It is a great burden to bear but the title of that play sums up the problem now facing a modern investigation.

Having lived with the case for some considerable time, I was as keen as anyone to try and uncover the killer's identity. I have gone over the evidence time and time again, and slowly but surely like Neil, eliminated suspects and travelled down some long and fruitless paths.

Who were the suspects?

First Bert Shaw; he was confirmed as having been in Sheffield, although the family believe Derby. In any event, he was far away from St Pauls Road.

Robert Percival Roberts, the ship's cook. The matter of the weapon will be considered again, but as a cook he could naturally wield a knife strong enough to slit a young girl's throat. At the time of the murder both his friend Frank Clark and his landlady confirm he was at his lodgings. Furthermore he was at the 'Rising Sun' on the 11th September, waiting to see if Emily would turn up. As it was, she was seen at the 'Eagle' in the company of Robert Wood.

Scotch Bob

'Scotch Bob'. The identity of this man, or of 'Scotty' has never been really clarified. John Crabtree considered him capable of murdering Emily, and had witnessed previous attacks on her. Marjoribanks states that 'Scotch Bob' was presented in court as a witness but he doesn't give him a name. He doesn't appear to be the Jack Carr apparently living in Belfast at the time.

In his own book, Sir David Napley offers an interesting story. 'Scotch Bob' turns out to be a man by the name of Mackie. The man who appeared in court was named John P Mair, who stated that Mackie was with him in Scotland on September 11th, and produced a document which helped fix the date. Napley's account is partly fictitious and he introduced names into his account that appear nowhere else, such as 'Gladys Warren', supposedly a previous landlady of Emily's. Therefore his version must be treated with caution such as the following.

On cross-examination of Mair, two dates were found on the document; one was 15th August and the other 15th September. Mair suggested that Mackie must have made a mistake but the issue was not taken any further, and the identity of 'Scotch Bob' and his whereabouts are as unclear as ever they were.

Henry Biddle who was believed to have married Emily in Portsmouth, and was one of the men said by Crabtree to have threatened her at 1, Bidborough Street, for having given him VD, was on the HMS Prince of Wales in Malta at the time of the murder.

As we know John Crabtree was in prison.

'Jumbo' Hurst

Of the main suspects one remains – 'Jumbo'.

I had tried for months to find out who 'Jumbo' was. He was obviously a big man to bear such a nickname. Its usage is said to have started from the introduction of an elephant to London Zoo. It was used to either reflect size, an ungainly walk or big ears. Many of the people involved in this murder worked on the railways, and doing idle searches on Google, I found that a Jumbo was a certain type of railway engine, called such because it was able to haul very heavy loads. This ran on the Midland Railway so I thought that 'Jumbo' might relate to an engine driver. Crabtree had also remarked that 'Scotch Bob' was a motor driver, and some engine drivers were called such. One of the references I found was to a picture that showed him driving 'RM no. 3' and that 'Hal's father was to become a Rail Motor driver'.

Then my enthusiasm ran riot for I found an account of the murder in a book already mentioned *Lust, Dust and Cobblestones* by Sue Fisher, which recounts folk lore and local colour from Hitchin and roundabouts.

The chapter mentions how the police called in a medium to help them with their investigation. The medium sat on the bed and 'then proceeded to give a startlingly vivid display of the actual commission of the crime, pictured in detail the appearance of a certain man and said, "The man you want is on his way to Melbourne." '

A few days later, I received from Bob Shaw a cutting from what he believes to be a Hertfordshire newspaper, and from which I have already mentioned Emily's father and sister. The report contains William Dimmock's own words as follows:

'She said (meaning Rosa) that she had already seen Emily in the spirit. On the day of the murder, at 3.00am Emily's spirit came to my bedside. I know the time because the clock struck three. I also saw the figure of Jumbo and I am sure he is the man who did it. His name is Large and he came down with her to Luton. In my vision I saw him get into a train and I seemed to be with him somehow, for when he got out there was a lot of water, and I saw him get into a ship.'

Rosa Martindale denied that she had been influenced by reports of the medium, but a suspicion must remain that she did not like Jumbo very much, and whatever happened when he and Emily visited her in 1906, she certainly thought him capable of serious harm to Emily.

I checked the ships to Melbourne for 'Large' and came up with nothing.

Taking this line of enquiry further, I searched for 'Jumbos' and other similar names and found on the 1901 census a Walter Large, aged 30, who was living in the St Pauls parish of Bedford, and was an engine driver on the Midland Railway.

Co-incidence and fantasy took over. Emily was employed at the Swan Hotel in Bedford and was taken away to London by her sister Maud when just 16. The Swan Hotel is also in the St Pauls parish, and could it be that Maud was trying to save her sister from the attentions of an older man – in 1902 Walter would have been 31.

It was too good to be true. Emily was killed in her home at 29 St Pauls Road.

With so many other co-incidences occurring this one seemed to fit. Anyone working on the railway could have been in the Kings Cross area almost at any time. Emily might have met Bert in London who was working as a chef for the same company, and the main line ran from St Pancras to Bedford – easy to get back home and disappear under a routine timetable.

Stranger things happen in life. On January 7th 2004, an 81 year old retired army colonel was found shot on his doorstep in the village of Furneaux (pronounced Furnix) Pelham. I am writing this in September 2005, and his killer has still not been found. In May of 2004, the local paper, the *Hertfordshire Mercury* published a report of an anonymous mystic who had driven through the village in October 2003, and had a notion that something terrible was going to happen.

He said to the *Mercury*: 'I told them things about the case which they said afterwards had not been released yet. I told him (the investigating officer) that the killer had gone abroad and would come back in two years time.'

Another little co-incidence to round off the story. When my wife and I were married in 1988, we had our reception in Furneaux Pelham, at the 'Star' public house; which has now been converted to a private residence.

I put this theory to some of my friends and it seemed to fit, until the police file was obtained. As we now know 'Jumbo' was Jumbo Hurst, a Grenadier Guardsman, nearly 6ft 3 inches in height, stationed at the Tower of London. Apart from the incident in which Robert Wood was seen running away from him, nothing more was known of Jumbo. Neil ascertained that he was married and dropped him from his investigations.

Sharples and Harvey

This leaves but two alternatives. One being the man seen by the pimps, Sharples and Harvey in the early hours of 12th September.

It is easy to understand Marshall Hall's frustration at not being able to call these two men as witnesses in court, and why he believed their testimony to be so important. Robert Wood was confirmed as to having returned home about midnight, so that the man with Emily would have been the last man to be seen with her and not Wood.

Hall's frustration was not just borne out by the sighting of these two men. Emily's landlady Mrs Stocks and a neighbour both confirmed that she left the house sometime between 8.00pm and 9.00pm on the evening of 12th September; the postcard to her sister Maud backs this up and she was later seen in the 'Eagle'.

Neil's investigations uncovered at least three other people who said they saw Emily in the Somers Town area of Kings Cross, between about 2.00pm and 4.00pm that afternoon. Bert would have left for work, so that Emily was left to her own devices. Of interest is that these witnesses state that Emily was walking arm in arm with a tall, fair man in a blue serge suit and bowler hat.

The dress code was normal for a white collar employee at the turn of the century, and as was well known Emily had many male friends, possibly what my mother might have called 'admirers'. The description given by Harry Sharples and Frederick Harvey matched the description of the man seen with Emily.

Neil dismissed the evidence of Sharples and Harvey

quite summarily. Although living off immoral earnings the men came forward voluntarily which is something in their favour; but many of Emily's lady friends did not recognise any of her male acquaintances from the description. Neil's reasoning that Emily was such a popular figure around Kings Cross that more than just Sharples and Harvey would have seen her, was the argument given by Charles Mathews for not calling them as witnesses for the prosecution.

The prosecution is duty bound to make all the evidence available to the defence. It can also choose not to call witnesses, but the defence can, although it must accept the witnesses statement without any right of cross examination. Marshall Hall maintained his assault on the decision not to call the two men, but was constantly overruled by Grantham who again rebuked him in his summing up. However, by his persistence, Marshall Hall may well have influenced the jury as well as if the men were questioned in the witness box.

Neil concluded by stating that it was of no matter whether Emily was seen out and about in the afternoon, because it was a matter of fact that she did go out in the evening to meet Robert Wood. Neil was entitled to his views, but the prosecution also had a right to see that justice was served and be seen to be served.

It is a matter of conjecture what might have happened had Sharples and Harvey been cross examined, but their social standing was no better than

This is Goods Way in December 2003, by day.

John Crabtree, and their own characters would have been blackened in court, if that was possible. Perhaps that was in the minds of the prosecution team.

Many writers have latched on to Marshall Hall's cross-examination of a female friend of Emily's who was hurt by one of his questions: 'You are trying to make me into a bad character.'

'God forbid,' remarked Hall, 'that I should make you one.'

The stranger

In Edwardian England, the majority of its citizens desired nothing more than respectability, and shied away from any association with men such as Crabtree, Sharples or Harvey. What credence would any such juror place on testimony from such as those.

The identity of the tall, fair man remains a mystery – as well as the woman believed to be Emily Dimmock. There remains one further possibility; that the murderer will remain as 'person or persons unknown'.

I have always thought it unkind to refer to Emily as a prostitute. There was no doubt she earned money from sex and had a string of lovers. But she was what so many of her kind were called in that age – an 'enthusiastic amateur'. There are less flattering modern terms – village bike, tart or local slapper. Given the Shaw's circumstances, it is more probable that all she was aiming to do was to supplement the household income, and give herself a bit of a good time into the bargain.

It is possible that Robert Wood left her outside the 'Eagle'. Or that they walked down Great College Street, under the railway arches that exit into Goods Way, where the red light district has now been submerged under the new Euro tunnel terminal, or to Somers Town, and into her usual stomping ground in the Euston Road. Robert Wood would walk on to Grays Inn Road, and his father's home in Frederick Street. Neither would meet each other again.

Perhaps alone again, Emily found a customer, someone she knew, or maybe a complete stranger who she took back to her rooms and who killed her. This is just supposition, and if a complete stranger it is certain his identity will never be known.

This is always an unsatisfactory ending, and why modern investigations continue to try and put a name to a suspect. This may well have been the end to the story if not for Patricia Cornwell and her book on Jack the Ripper.

Was Emily Dimmock a Ripper victim?

6 WAS EMILY DIMMOCK A RIPPER VICTIM?

In attempting to answer this question, one problem springs to mind. Why was there a gap of nineteen years between the murder of Mary Kelly and Emily Dimmock? Surely a serial killer kills and then kills again until he is caught, or dies? Rarely do they wait for nineteen years to strike again. Yet this is what Patricia Cornwell would have us believe.

I am not an expert on Jack the Ripper, the Whitechapel murders or any of the conspiracy theories. I have read quite a few, and like so many have a lifelong fascination for the Ripper. My father's family came from Hoxton, now gentrified, but then a poor working class area close to Whitechapel. I can't remember anyone in the family ever suggesting that Walter Sickert could be the Ripper. I think, like so many people, they would like him to have been the Duke of Clarence, because there is nothing like a bit of royal scandal to liven up a conversation. Why then has Sickert become the prime suspect in so many people's minds and what connects him to Emily Dimmock?

The first part of this poser is relatively complex, and for anyone really interested in following the various strands of the conspiracies, and the involvement of the Royal family and the Freemasons, then there is a select bibliography at the end of this book. However, this is the edited version.

The Conspiracy Theory

Walter Sickert rented many studios. One was in Cleveland Street, which has been mentioned before in regards to Arthur Newton. In Cleveland Street, there was a tobacconists at which a girl named Annie Crook worked. She caught the eye of Edward, Duke of Clarence, and fell pregnant by him. They went through a form of marriage in a Catholic church in Walworth (where many people have placed Emily's birth as well). This was the epicentre of the scandal, that the illegitimate heir to the throne was Catholic.

Annie Crook was kidnapped, and placed in a lunatic asylum where she died; but not until after William Gull, the Queen's surgeon had performed some very nasty experiments on her.

Walter Sickert's father was German and had connections with the royal family. Sickert became a friend of the Duke of Clarence, and of Queen Victoria herself. Sickert undertook to take care of Annie's child and employed two nursemaids; one was his mistress Florence Pash and the other Mary Kelly.

Mary Kelly accompanied Sickert to Dieppe but soon returned to London and the East End. The illegitimate daughter had been taken away from Annie Crook and was not heard of again. Mary Kelly was the one person outside of the royal circle who knew all this. It was a dangerous thing to know.

Sickert's loyalty was to the throne and the royal family. Mary Kelly was blackmailing him, and had apparently leaked out her secret to her friends who were prostitutes in the Whitechapel area.

To protect the secret, Sickert embarked upon an orgy of killing and murdered all of Mary Kelly's friends, culminating in the atrocious mutilation of Mary herself. Thus having prevented a royal scandal and secured the Protestant accession, Sickert stopped, and with him Jack the Ripper. Until for no apparent reason he killed Emily Dimmock?

Was Walter Sickert Jack the Ripper? Very possibly. Although in the latest version of her book, *Sickert and the Ripper Crimes* Jean Overton Fuller believes that Sickert was only responsible for the murder of Mary Kelly to protect the royal family, and possibly Catherine Eddowes whom he mistook for Mary in the dark.

There is also some doubt as to whether the body

found in 26 Dorset Street was that of Mary. Her body was so mutilated identification was impossible; even her common law husband was unable to recognise her except for the colour of her hair and eyes. Despite there being some inconsistencies even then his word was considered good enough.

Those with a knowledge of the case will know that there was a sighting of Mary Kelly the next morning by one of her drinking friends. The latter was said to be drunk and had mistaken the date. In many Ripper books, it is claimed that Sickert continued to receive letters from an address in Ireland; many believe that they were from Mary Kelly who had settled there, to continue to look after the illegitimate heir to the throne. Having a body so torn apart as to be unidentifiable would be the perfect cover under which to smuggle the real person out of the country.

And the other Ripper victims?

When a modern murder scene develops, the police only release the details that they believe are necessary. Many facts are suppressed that would only be known to the killer. There were no such restrictions in 1888. The press were free to report what they wanted, and to glamorise or sensationalise whenever the story appeared to need it.

Life was cheap in the latter part of the nineteenth century, especially in the East End where starvation was a constant companion. It is possible that the Ripper murders were domestic quarrels that had escalated into mindless violence, or copycat killings lifted from the pages of the popular press. I do not offer this as a solution, just as something to consider.

Was Emily Dimmock a Ripper victim?

Highly improbable. The Ripper first cut his victim's throat, and then tore open their vital organs leaving them in a pool of blood, and in a few cases departing with body parts to dispose of later.

The only similarity with Emily's murder was that her throat was cut. It is not an easy way to kill someone. It is an easier suicide option. An intentional murderous attack has to come from behind, and the approach made silently or else the victim has time to struggle, to put up a fight and the cut is rarely clean. There are cuts all over the arms and upper torso, possibly on the face from fighting off the assailant. The act is even more difficult if the murder is done face to face, because the element of surprise is missing and the victim has more time to defend themselves.

The Ripper victims all had their throats cut, which might presume that they were caught unawares, that their killer came from behind. Emily was asleep when she was murdered; in a perfect situation for someone to attack her without warning and without defence.

But more important, Emily's body was found in her

bed; she was killed as she slept, and there was no further attempts at mutilation, although in that closed room her killer would have had plenty of time to do as he wished. Her killer actually washed his hands and dried them leaving the room almost undisturbed.

Ms Cornwell has said that serial killers have a pattern, they leave their trademark almost as a fingerprint. There was no trademark left in Emily's room. Whoever her killer was, it was not the same man that terrorised the East End.

Walter Sickert

And for the second part of the question: what connects Sickert to Emily Dimmock?

There is no mention of Walter Sickert in Inspector Neil's report. He was never questioned as being an acquaintance or client of Emily's, or of being a suspect. None of Emily's friends mention her association with an artist, apart from describing her long association with Robert Wood.

To have been able to sketch the death bed scene for the series of paintings named after the crime, Sickert would have had to have been in the house some time. Bert Shaw was the first to enter the room, and up until Emily's body was removed the only other people to enter were family or police.

Just believe for a moment the evidence of Sharples and Harvey. If the last person seen with Emily was in her company at about 12.30am, the description does not match that of Sickert. She could have left this man and picked up a stranger – a 'person unknown' and this could have been Sickert. It is a short walk from the Kings Cross arches, along Crowndale Road to Mornington Crescent, but why would Sickert want to go all the way up York Way, or even St Pancras Way to St Paul's Road, when his own studio was closer.

In one of many letters to me, whilst we were exchanging notes on her revised book, Miss Fuller states that Florence Pash, Sickert's mistress told her mother that she did not think he committed the Camden Town Murder. This is explained further a little later.

The one real connection between Walter Sickert and Emily Dimmock are the paintings now known as the Camden Town Murder series, and in particular the canvas later renamed 'What shall we do for the rent'. It is thought that the woman lying on the bed was inspired by Emily Dimmock, but was intended to be Mary Kelly.

Many of Sickert's paintings of this period were set in music halls, and in particular the Old Bedford Music Hall in Camden High Street. My parents used to go there every week. It was a popular venue – all the leading stars played there, from Marie Lloyd to George Robey, who had a pub named after him just a mile or two up the road at Finsbury Park. The Bedford was

The Old Bedford Music Hall, prior to 1939.

bombed during the Second World War, and after being rebuilt in the fifties and experiencing a brief renaissance it became derelict, until finally being demolished in 1969.

Whilst I was growing up in Camden, it was more like a great big hole in the street; there were so many such bombed out areas, you half expected a car park to be built on top. Instead, it remained a local landmark and a bus stop was named after it. My mother still asked bus drivers to stop outside the Bedford, but they were born far too young to know what she was talking about.

During her final years, I wrote a history of the Bedford in the hope that publication would help my mother through her growing dementia. By the time it was published, she was 91, and died just afterwards. However, it was by placing this article on my website that it was seen by Alan Stanley, and I first became aware of the Camden Town Murder.

Emily Dimmock must also have visited the Bedford. It would have been the closest place of entertainment after the local pubs. I am not suggesting that she would have met Sickert on one of her visits, but one of the false trails I passed down involved Walter Large who lived in the St Pauls area of Bedford. It seemed a co-incidence too far.

One way or the other, the murder of Emily Dimmock had a huge effect on Walter Sickert. He was living close to the murder scene, and would have known all about the police investigation from the local press and his circle of friends. It was an horrific crime and must have drawn some similarity with the Ripper crimes.

It is not necessary to believe that Sickert was Jack the Ripper. Many people do and much has been written on the subject, including that written by Jean Overton Fuller. Her book recounts the story of Walter Sickert and his connection to the Ripper killings as told by Florence Pash, Sickert's mistress, to Miss Fuller's mother. This is what she wrote to me in 2002:

'My only info regarding that is that Florence Pash told my mother and my mother told me in 1948 that Sickert's paintings of the Camden Town Murder were not in fact of the Camden Town Murder but of his recollections of the dreadful bleeding bodies of 1888, which never for one day or hour of his life left his mind. It may well be – probably is – only that calling the paintings Camden Town Murder allowed him to regurgitate on to canvas his memories of what happened in 1888.'

If this was so, then this will explain the discussion in artistic circles as to the identity of the woman lying on the bed. Many have thought this was Mary Kelly, others that it was Emily Dimmock. The original title was the Camden Town Murder but later Sickert (as he did with many of his works) renamed it: 'What shall we do for the rent'.

Emily Dimmock was not behind with her rent, Mary Kelly was and there the matter would rest, but for other similarities with both.

In 1907, there was no Social Security, no minimum wage, no safety net for the unemployed or unemployable, no State aid, and the only people who you could turn to for cash were the moneylenders. There was really only one way for many women to make ends meet – to sell their body for a 'twopenny knee trembler' against any convenient brick wall. These were the type of women murdered by Jack the Ripper.

Prostitution is too strong a word for what these women did. Dictionaries of Slang are full of terms for these 'enthusiastic amateurs'. One of these was Emily Dimmock. She lived quite comfortably in two rooms, in a reasonably pleasant part of North London, despite the railways rattling through the neighbourhood. She had a husband in all but name who had a good job with a decent weekly pay packet, and she had many of the trappings of domesticity.

Why then would Emily turn to working on the streets? It is possible that her immoral or irresponsible behaviour was partly a result of her fall in childhood, and had affected her mental powers. More likely, the reason was in the Shaw's household budget.

This is from Neil's report: 'Careful enquiries show that when Shaw first knew this woman he knew perfectly well that she was leading a very debased life. When he took up his residence with her he was only earning 18s(hillings) a week (pre1971 old currency). Out of this sum they were paying 8s. for rent, 2s.6d for the hire of a piano, 1s. 3d. for furniture and 1s. 6d. for a sewing machine. These outgoings, it will be seen, amount to 13s. 3d. a week, leaving 4s.9d. out of his salary for pocket money for himself and keep for them both, and it was only about two months earlier that he began to earn 27s. per week.

It is also well known that she has bought him several suits of clothes since he has been living with her.'

Neil mentions elsewhere that Bert did more than 'wink' at Emily's part-time occupation.

The 'Shaws' were living beyond their means; not so dissimilar to many couples even in the twenty first century. The Royal Furnishing Company wrote to the Metropolitan Police on 18 December 1907, requesting the return of their rented goods since 'Mr Shaw had failed to fulfil the terms of his Agreement' with them. Listed were: 4' bedstead, p[air]r palliasses, bed (mattress presumably), bolster, 2 pillows, 16 sq yards floorcloth, polished chest, 3 chairs, 16 yards floorcloth, rug, p[ai]r second-hand blankets and slip mats.

They appeared to be in some debt. Unlike modern couples there was little else to do; they could not re-mortgage their house, extend the overdraft or apply for a loan. There was only one thing for it – Emily had to earn money as best she could. All accounts and contemporary photographs show Emily to be an attractive, vivacious young woman with an ear for music. She would not have found it difficult to attract clients.

In Sickert's painting we see a woman lying naked on the bed, a man sitting on the side looking despondent. There is nothing to say these are not a married couple asking each other the question that couples all over the country ask in times of economic depression and hardship: 'What shall we do for the rent'. The painting is really a comment on the social mores of the time, something with which many married men and women could empathise.

This book does not seek to answer the question as to whether Walter Sickert was Jack the Ripper, but I doubt if he was the killer of Emily Dimmock. Which still leaves the vital question unanswered – who was?

7 WHO DID KILL
   EMILY DIMMOCK?

By now the reader may have become as frustrated as the writer in trying to identify the suspect. There were so many men who could have committed this murder. It appears, as even Judge Grantham noted in his summing up, a motiveless crime. This may be the case, and might have remained so, but for the research and work carried out by a forensic pathologist which was passed backwards and forwards between us for comment and evaluation.

I am indebted to Paul Brooks for all this work and much of this chapter is based on his findings. As much as Alan Stanley initially opened the door to me, Paul turned on the light.

The division in social class was remarked upon in Chapter Four. Witnesses for the prosecution that came from the lower classes were subject to any manner of character assassination; and it was expected.

Time of death

One witness and one piece of evidence was never questioned - Dr John Thompson and his estimation of time of death.

The findings of doctors were usually taken as being one hundred per cent correct, even though medical experts were inclined to speculate rather more than they were entitled. Owing to their status they were rarely challenged, and much rested upon what they said even though it was very often unsubstantiated guesswork.

When PC Thomas Killion arrived at the scene at 12.00 noon on 12 September 1907, he found Emily Dimmock 'dead and cold'. The Police Surgeon Dr Thompson arrived at 1.00pm, and in his statement he says that she had been dead for 6-7 hours. At the inquest he suggested this was 7-8 hours.

Thompson said that when he examined Emily's body at 1.00pm she was 'cold and rigid – rigor mortis had set in'. Simpson's *Forensic Medicine* gives a rule of thumb for such a crude estimate of time of death, under average conditions as follows; although 'cold' and 'stiff' can only be relative and subjective terms:

1. Body feels warm and flaccid – dead for

less than three hours

2. Body warm and stiff – dead 3-8 hours
3. Body cold and stiff – dead for 8-36 hours
4. Body cold and flaccid – dead for more than 36 hours.

Rigor mortis is the stiffening of the muscles caused by chemical changes occurring in the body following death. Every muscle in the body undergoes rigor mortis. Stiffening begins within two to five hours after death. The entire body will be rigid within 12 to 18 hours of death. Thereafter, rigor mortis begins to dissipate and, within another 18 hours, the rigor mortis will disappear and the body will again, resume a relaxed state.

It is also dependent on the temperature and metabolic rate. At 70-75°Fahrenheit, rigor mortis will start to set in after one hour. After 10-12 hours the body will be in complete rigor mortis and remain so for 24-36 hours.

September 1907 was an exceptionally warm month. September 11th, was one of the warmest – about 77° Fahrenheit (25° Celsius). Much was made of MacCowan's statement, that the morning of the 12th was drizzly, thick and muggy. All of these could apply, but it was certainly warm and rigor would have set in just a little bit more quickly.

Thompson could not have tied down the time of

death so precisely. He probably tried to give a more accurate estimate by using the state of the stomach, but he would also need to know when she ate her last meal.

Thompson found the remains of a partly digested meal of lamb and potatoes in Emily's stomach and concluded the meal had been eaten some 3-3½ hours prior to death. This was based on hearsay evidence, that she was in the habit of eating her supper at around 11.30pm, and thus concluded that the time of death was 3am. There was no evidence to say when she ate her last meal, and the condition of the stomach contents is well known to be a poor guide to estimating time elapsed before death.

Dismissing the stomach contents as a guide, Emily could have died any time between when she was last seen alive at 9.30pm on the previous evening in the 'Eagle' and realistically a minimum of eight hours before she was found. This is based on the body being cold and stiff between 8 and 36 hours after death. She was discovered at 11.30am, so the latest time could be 3.30am giving a window of 6 hours in which no one can positively describe her movements.

Only Sir David Napley comments on the lack of cross examination of Dr Thompson. Why did neither prosecution or defence counsel attempt to discredit his evidence?

As stated above, the art of forensic science was not

yet established, and the findings of the medical profession were rarely if ever questioned. However, both counsel would have had their own reasons for not wanting the time of death altered from between 3.00am and 5.00am.

First of all the prosecution. They had a witness, Robert MacCowan, who would testify that he saw a man fitting Robert Wood's description, leave 29 St Pauls Road just before 5.00am. Although his testimony was challenged in the magistrates courts at the pre-trial hearings, the prosecution still had a man leaving the premises that they felt they could establish was Wood by the nature of his walk. A fact later corroborated by Ruby Young. It was not until Newton found William Westcott on the eve of the trial that the man's identity was established. Westcott also stated that he kept in his sights a man heading north towards Brewery Road, and that man was established as Robert MacCowan.

It was the cornerstone of Marshall Hall's defence that at the time of death as testified by Dr Thompson his client Robert Wood was at home. In fact many of the other suspects also had alibis that confirmed them as having been at home or at their lodgings, in bed asleep at the time of the murder. Marshall Hall would not have wanted the time of death changed and saw no reason to challenge the medical testimony.

If the time of death was much earlier, from any time after 9.30pm, then Robert Wood's alibi is less secure.

He said he arrived home at about midnight, a fact confirmed by his father, step brother and lodger. But he had already asked his former lover Ruby Young and then Joseph Lambert to lie for him, so why not those closer to him? He may only have needed a half hour, but that would have been enough to keep him out of the time frame of the murder; which only the murderer would have known.

The last person to see Emily with Robert Wood was the barmaid at the 'Eagle', Lilian Raven, who said they had been in the pub until about 9.30pm. Wood said that they parted outside but maybe not.

Mrs Stocks the landlady at 29 St Pauls Road, said that she and her husband, who also worked on the railway, went to bed early, between about 10.00pm and 11.00pm. She claims not to have been aware of Emily's night time activities. It is difficult to believe this unless they were very heavy sleepers.

Emily had moved around from one rented room to another, possibly at the behest of the landlord if her profession became too obvious. The Stocks would not want it known that Emily was using her rooms to entertain paying clients. It would ruin the Stocks reputation, and possibly lead to a police investigation for keeping 'a disorderly house' bringing them down to the same level as John Crabtree.

It is more likely that she, like Bert, turned a blind eye as long as the rent was paid and Emily did not make things too obvious. She did not speak ill of Emily and it must have been difficult not to ignore the movements every night coming from above – the Stocks lived on the ground floor, although we might call it the basement – knowing full well that Bert was away at work.

On the day after the murder she was interviewed by the *Northampton Herald* and called the Shaws her 'newly married couple in the parlour-set'. A fine piece of middle class snobbery if ever there was one. She continued:

> 'Emily was a most proper and well-spoken
> young person, kind to everybody, quiet, and
> not given to gallivanting about. Indeed the pair
> seemed very happy, and in the afternoons
> when Shaw was away she used to amuse her-
> self by singing and playing the piano. She was
> always nicely and neatly dressed with a pleas-
> ant face, and quite good manners.'

Either the Stocks were living in blissful ignorance, or Mrs Stocks had a very nice line in hypocrisy.

It is a short, about a five minutes walk from the 'Eagle' to St Pauls Road. As long as they made no unnecessary noise, they just had to let themselves in through the front door, the Stocks' bedroom possibly at the back of the house under Emily's own. Neither the Stocks nor any of the other lodgers mention hearing anyone enter the house during the night. However, Emily seems to have been adept at taking men back to lodgings without making anyone aware. By 10.00pm Emily and Wood might have been sitting down to what was her last meal of lamb and potatoes.

Whoever Emily did bring back to her room that night she knew well. Her hair was still in curling pins and she then ate a meal, had sex with him and drifted into sleep. This is not the actions of a frightened woman or of one entertaining a stranger. Nor would it appear that she returned alone and let someone in.

She could have been killed at any time between about 10.30pm and 03.00am. Bert Shaw noticed that several personal items were missing – a silver cigarette case, a silver curb chain with a vesta case and charm attached that belonged to him, a purse with about five shillings inside, a gold watch, a gold wedding ring, and a gold curb ring that belonged to Emily. Also missing were her keys. We know that Bert had no keys as he couldn't let himself in and borrowed a spare set from Mrs Stocks.

Whoever was in the room with Emily either stole some personal items to make it look like a robbery; then took her keys to ensure only Bert would be able to get in to find her. Bert's working hours were the reason that Emily could carry on as she did, so his movements must have been quite common knowledge. Or she was killed for the few pennies that could be

The Eagle public house is just past the bridge.

raised on the items. Although Bert was sure of what was missing, Emily was no stranger to the pawn shop but as no redeemable tickets were found we have to go along with the robbery.

The killer then rifled through what few possessions were left; the photograph album was the main object of attention. Some postcards could have been removed, but the killer also left some other items of jewellery so it is difficult to ascertain exactly what he was looking for.

Bert Shaw stated that the shutters were usually closed at night, yet when he entered the room they were slightly open. The reports make no mention if any lights were on; if not, then Emily and her killer finished their meal and then turned off the lights. Or they could have been left on for the killer to watch over Emily as she slept and have light by which to kill her. Then extinguished it as surely as Emily's life. The shutters might have been opened to check to see if the coast was clear; or possibly not closed properly that evening. There is no way of knowing these 97 years later.

The streets around the area might still have been busy until past midnight, the pubs were emptying and many people still walking home. No one would have given a second thought to a man leaving number 29 St Pauls Road at 11.30pm or slightly later. The police had not asked for witnesses and when they did it was for the early hours of 12th September that interested them; the approximate time of death as stated by Dr Thompson. As it was, Robert MacCowan came forward but what might have been the response if sightings had been requested for much earlier.

This is just supposition for the killer could make his escape in any direction. North towards York Way, west along Murray Street to Camden Road, or south to Great College Street. Whatever direction he chose he would have been quickly swallowed up in the residential streets of North London.

By re-assessing the time of death, Robert Wood's alibi, his requests to his lover and his friend and his lies, paint a very different scenario to one who only lied to save his family from shame and embarrassment.

From St Pauls Road to Grays Inn Road is about a mile – or about twenty minutes brisk walk. It is easier going that way as it is downhill. There are two main approaches. Up St Pauls Road, turn right at the crossroads to York Way, and then straight down to Kings Cross.

Alternatively turn right from No.29, and then left at St Pancras Way. When I was a boy this was commonly known as Fire Engine Hill because there was a Fire Station near the top; but also excellent to race soap boxes down as long as you had good brakes when you hit the bottom. Turn left and you walk past St Pancras Church, under the railway arches and into Kings Cross

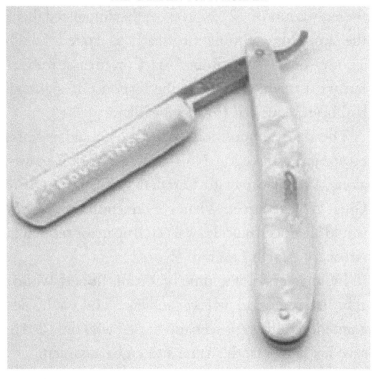

A typical cut-throat razor.

and the junction with St Pancras Station. Ahead is the Euston Road.

Assuming Robert Wood arrived home at about midnight, he would have left Emily at about 11.40pm; having murdered her about fifteen minutes or so earlier, with time to clean up and search her rooms. His false alibi would now no longer be of use for he claimed it was to prevent his family knowing of his association with Emily. Once the murder can be fixed much earlier almost anyone could have committed the crime, including Wood. It also means that the evidence of Sharples and Harvey is flawed. Emily was already dead when they claimed to have seen her with the tall, blond man in the blue serge suit. Possibly a classic case of mistaken identity.

The weapon

The change in time of death is sufficient to give Robert Wood opportunity. But what of the murder weapon?

Thompson thought that a razor had been used, but only perhaps because there were razors in the room. There was no evidence that either had been used. A cut throat razor is not the ideal weapon to use because it is not rigid. It is undoubtedly sharp but it would not be regarded as strong enough blade to inflict the single cut across her throat from ear to ear. The cut was almost down to the spine and severed major vessels on

161

that side and cut through the windpipe, so that she would have been unable to make a sound.

The only weapon that could inflict that kind of injury is a large sharp, perhaps double bladed knife. It is not the kind of instrument that many people carry about with them, unless they actually intend to commit a serious crime.

Paul Brooks believed it could have been a kind of knife used by a chef, or someone who was used to using wielding such a blade in the course of their work. The two men that spring to mind are Bert Shaw and Robert Roberts, both cooks; one on the railway, one on the ship.

However Bert was in Sheffield and Roberts was in the 'Rising Sun' until late waiting for Emily, and then returned home.

There is no record of such a knife being found in Emily's room. Either the killer came prepared with his own knife or found such a knife at the scene, and in cool presence of mind took it with him.

There is no mention in the police report of any other knives being found. Bert Shaw was a cook, and may have prepared meals at home and possessed such a knife needed to slice through any manner of meat. It would have needed to have been of exceptional sharpness.

In these modern times, nearly everything can be bought at the supermarket – many on the outskirts of

A typical knife-grinder with barrow.

our towns and cities have become one-stop megastores. At the turn of the century most tradesmen and sellers of foodstuffs came to the customer. My father fondly recalled a pie man in the East End who carried his wares through the streets, and his customers had to keep up a steady walking/running pace in order to buy them. The pie man never stood still. The only tradesman nowadays to deliver to your door is the milkman, and even that last vestige of personal service is fast fading in the face of price competition from the supermarkets.

Amongst the coal merchants, the sweep, the rag and bone man, the baker, the organ-grinder with his performing monkey, and the many other tradesmen to be found in the streets, was the knife-grinder and his well-known call: 'Knives to grind'. All manner of household implements could be sharpened by the man on his large three wheeled bike, with the large granite stone wheel. Knives, scissors and garden tools were just a few. It was not improbable that any knife found in an Edwardian kitchen would have had a much keener blade than any found in a modern semi-detached.

Is it possible that the sensitive graphic artist such as Robert Wood was capable of wielding such a dangerous weapon? This was not a frenzied attack with multiple stab wounds; this was one single cut made with precision. The murderer did not lash out with a sharp knife indiscriminately at any part of the body. He lifted up Emily's head from the pillow where she was sleeping, pushed back her hair, adjusted the position of her arm and just nicking the sheet with the blade cut cleanly through her throat.

What kind of man would perform such a cold crime? Charles Mathews was in no doubt that this was just the kind of man Robert Wood was. It was because he was so cold blooded that he was able to remain calm and lie in the face of the police investigation, and to remain so in court.

There is a strange passage in Edward Marjoribanks book on the trials of Marshall Hall. He says of Wood's description of Emily as a 'crushed rose that had not lost all of its fragrance' that 'it was almost as if he had been reading 'Jenny' by Dante Gabriel Rossetti'.

This is the opening verse of 'Jenny':
Lazy laughing languid Jenny,
Fond of a kiss and fond of a guinea,
Whose head upon my knee to-night
Rests for a while, as if grown light
With all our dances and the sound
To which the wild tunes spun you round:
Fair Jenny mine, the thoughtless queen
Of kisses which the blush between
Could hardly make much daintier;
Whose eyes are as blue skies, whose hair
Is countless gold incomparable:

Fresh flower, scarce touched with signs that
tell
Of Love's exuberant hotbed:—Nay,
Poor flower left torn since yesterday
Until to-morrow leave you bare;
Poor handful of bright spring-water
Flung in the whirlpool's shrieking face;

This is a poem of great contrast, between the controlling male and the passive female. This is accentuated by Jenny's servile position, sleeping on the narrator's knee, he looking down at her. There is no doubt that Jenny is a prostitute and is desired by the narrator but that such a profession is immoral. Once again in late Victorian society we have the problems facing men such as Robert Wood of living a so called respectable life during the day but driven by desire for the seedy side of life by night.

I do not know if Marjoribanks intended to make a strong comparison but the link between Rossetti and Jenny, and Wood and Emily is a hard one not to ignore. The image of Jenny lying asleep on the narrator's knee is similar to the killer holding up Emily's head before slitting her throat.

Motive

The next question to be asked is how Robert Wood could have acquired such knowledge to have ended

Emily's life in such a way. It will be recalled, that on leaving school he earned a living for a short while as steward at the Australian Members Club at University College. Whilst there he made some money copying medical and anatomical drawings for students. This would have given him an ideal grounding in the workings of the human body, and the knowledge of the best way to immediately silence and then kill, another human being.

From many contemporary reports Wood had a temper. The window cleaner Miller testified that he had been threatening Emily before 'Jumbo' Hurst arrived to break them up. John Crabtree also stated that he had seen Wood threaten Emily on more than one occasion and ask for money. This was not the Robert Wood that would have been recognisable by his employers.

There is nothing in any reports that Robert Wood was in debt. He had a good position and no doubt a more than average salary, but Crabtree insists that on occasions he had demanded money from Emily. Mathews interpretation of the charred letter found in the grate was that the letters 'mon' referred to money. Many of Emily's and Bert's valuables were missing from their rooms but the killer also left behind some rings.

That charred letter was shown to Roberts by Emily who told him that it was sent to her by a man she referred to as 'Bert'. In his letter from prison to his brother, Wood had signed himself 'Bob'. Roberts had told Neil that this was the man he had seen in conversation with her at the 'Rising Sun' public house the previous Monday night.

Emily also told Roberts he was a man of whom she was very much afraid. This man, she said, was at that time pressed for money which he only received once a month. He came from a good family, and if she allowed him to sleep with her he would redeem all her valuables then in pawn.

Roberts maintained that this was the man he had seen Emily argue with in the 'Rising Sun' on the Monday night, and about whom she had told her women friends that she 'had made it alright with him'.

All we have to verify this relationship is Roberts' word. It was either a truthful recollection of their conversations, or Roberts was 'gilding the lily' after the event to clear himself from any involvement by blackening Robert Wood. The only way he would have known is if Emily had connected the letter, the postcard, the man 'Bert' and a description of Robert Wood together. How else would Roberts have been able to make the same connection?

Everything is pure supposition. Robert Wood may have owed people money; David Napley infers that he tried to pay for Emily's services with a cigarette case, on which he asked Crabtree to raise money, but as stated in the last chapter Napley employed a vivid imagination. No one is confident about the cause of the arguments between Emily and Wood, and if robbery was a motive there was certainly no need to have committed murder for what would have been a trifling sum.

Robert Wood's father George was by then 67 and a sick man. According to Michael Cotgrove (see earlier note) the illness was temporary and he was still working as a printer's compositor. One of the words Charles Mathews extrapolated from the remains of the letter was 'ill'. Robert had been to Bruges earlier in the year. The famous 'Rising Sun' postcard had apparently been purchased in Bruges. Robert Wood too, like the Shaws, could have been living well beyond his means; supporting himself, his father and paying good money to indulge his night time interests.

Whatever Wood's financial situation, and there is little contemporary evidence to make any assumption, it is clear that he had the opportunity, the time, the weapon and means to kill Emily Dimmock but we are left with the last piece of the puzzle; as to why?

In addition to the postcard, three other postcards were found in Emily's photograph album which appear to be in the same handwriting.

The postmark on one shows it to have been posted at Brighton on January 9th, one other in January, but the rest of the postmark was indistinct; and the other posted at Windsor on August 19th. The first two were addressed to Mrs Shaw, 30 Great College Street and the other at 29 St Pauls Road. The writer had a good knowledge of her movements and was certainly known to her since January last.

Were these the items for which her killer ransacked Emily's room; along with the letter and postcard? In any event, none of these items were discovered. Neil's contention was that they were all in the same handwriting. A detailed forensic examination by a modern graphology expert may have confirmed this, but there was not universal education at the time, and the clear script may have been well beyond the capability of many of the people interviewed and asked to give an example of their handwriting.

If indeed it was Robert Wood who searched unsuccessfully for the postcards, why was it necessary to do so? The only reason was that the acknowledgement of authorship would link him to Emily. In fact, as it eventually did so, when the postcard was published in the national newspapers and recognised by Ruby Young.

The postcard was well hidden as it was not found by Bert until leaving for other rooms and the letter had been partially burnt although recovered by the police. The killer could not have remained long in the room once the murder had been committed, or a more thorough search might have been made. Having made his escape all that was needed was to establish an alibi, made considerably easier once the time of death had been placed at 3.00am.

It is unlikely that robbery was the motive because other valuables were left; the postcard album was ransacked, possibly in an attempt to disguise his identity. The table showed the remains of a meal for two. A casual robber would not have been invited in, sat down for a meal, had sex, and then stole what he could after committing a cold blooded act of murder.

Emily was said by many of her friends to be afraid of the man possibly thought to be 'Scotch Bob' but sometimes seen in her company, and now known to be Robert Wood. She could have been blackmailing him but this seems very much out of character, and there would have been no need for her to say she was afraid if she had a hold on him. She may well have been afraid of his temper but the terms of their relationship, although having been maintained over a period of possibly eighteen months or more, remains shrouded in mystery.

Many of Emily's previous male friends had caught VD from her. At the time of her death she was clear. However, a few retained a level of hatred for her and threatened revenge. At the turn of the century it was a common complaint, and although the treatment was harsh not many actually died from the disease. It was not terminal.

There was nothing noted that Wood had contracted VD from Emily or anyone else. He was apparently in good health so a motive borne out of revenge does not seem possible.

One of the last remaining reasons is the likelihood that Robert Wood had become jealous. Emily had been his constant lover for some time; either for payment or from some form of physical attachment. He had often been kind about her. Marjoribanks says that Wood had written about Emily after the trial;

'She seemed a girl who might have seen better days, who might have made a good wife in other circumstances. It delighted me to sit with and talk to her. She was in herself an exceedingly attractive girl. She had a sort of rough refinement. I was not in love with her. She appealed in some way to my sense of the artistic.'

Marjoribanks does not give a source for this but it comes in the same paragraphs as the association with Rossetti and the poem 'Jenny'.

Yet in court when in the witness box and asked if Emily was wearing curling pins, he replied that he would not allow himself to be seen in public with a girl with hair like that. A strange comment from a man that two witnesses confirmed was with him on the night of

11th September. It was nothing less than a denial of any feelings he may have had.

Emily took some pride in her appearance, yet on the night of 11th September, rushed out in curling pins. This is not the action of a young woman going out to meet a lover, but more like a housewife rushing out to catch the last post. Did she have a change of mind and decide at the final moment to meet Robert Wood?

Whatever was in her mind that night, since the beginning of 1907 and possibly earlier, she had been living with Bert Shaw. It was a permanent, stable relationship. Emily had just turned 22, but Bert was still a minor. Nevertheless, they were contemplating marriage, for the consent forms from his parents had been signed despite some initial concerns from his father. Wedding plans were obviously advanced, for when William Dimmock visited the Shaws in August he mentioned that 'they were getting ready, so Mrs Shaw told me to get married.'

They had already set up home in St Pauls Road, and this may have been too much for Robert Wood. He had enjoyed Emily on and off over a long period, and even though she still returned to the streets, she had obviously committed herself to Bert rather than Wood by virtue of her impending marriage vows.

Wood's jealousy would have been simmering for a long time, almost a year. Was it a case of if I can't have her, no one can. As above this was not a killing executed in a jealous rage, in the heat of the moment after a fearful row. It was a premeditated, precision murder that deserved the death penalty.

In the absence of jealousy as a prime motive there can be little else a modern investigator can make of the reasons for Emily's murder. If she was an embarrassment then it would be easy just not to see her again. Wood had dropped Ruby Young in similar circumstances. Emily does not appear to be the clinging, possessive kind. She had men at her feet and one at home; and if rumour is anything to go by was owed more by Wood than the other way round.

There is therefore some grounds for attributing a motive to Robert Wood; one of jealousy. There is no one else who had opportunity, time, weapon, method and motive, and placed before a modern court and jury I believe that a verdict of guilty would have been found against Robert Wood.

He had enjoyed a lengthy relationship with Emily whilst she had been at other addresses; and now she was contemplating marriage. Many people had witnessed his temper. The thought of losing Emily altogether may have proved too much for him, linked to her continued association with other men, which finally pushed him over the brink into murder.

On the balance of the evidence Judge Grantham had no option but to direct the jury to acquit. Wood could not be placed at the scene of the crime and he had an alibi for the time of the murder. However modern forensic science not available in 1907, may have destroyed his alibi by determining the time of death, and providing DNA samples to place him at the scene of crime.

Almost 100 years later Robert Wood remains the prime suspect and in the mind of the author, guilty of the murder of Emily Dimmock.

As it was, he was acquitted to the disappointment of Inspector Neil. He wrote on 21 December 1907 to his superiors:

'Everything possible was done during the enquiry by myself and the officers acting under me to secure sufficient evidence to shew the prisoner's guilt.

The case was a most difficult and complicated one and the coolness exercised by the murderer, whoever he might have been, was most remarkable; and, as must be admitted, this made my task a very arduous one.

But, taking the whole of the circumstances into consideration I venture to express the opinion that nothing further can be done in the matter as we must abide by the jury's decision, although morally (?) there can be no doubt of the guilt of the accused man.'

So let the last word rest with Emily Dimmock. On her death certificate dated 1ˢᵗ November 1907, the registrar has written: 'Symarpe(?)[1] due to loss of blood from injuries to throat inflicted with some sharp instrument. Wilful murder against Robert William Thomas George Cavers Wood.'

Notes

1   I still cannot make out this word. Possibly synapse but does not fit, and *Shorter Oxford English Dictionary* says word is rare of obsolete. The word 'syncope' to mean 'to faint' has also been suggested. What is clear is that death was induced by a sharp weapon.

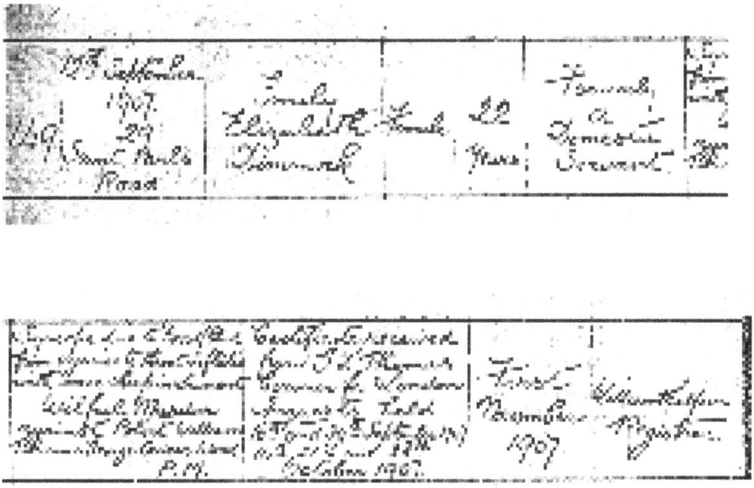

Emily's Death Certificate.

8 AFTERMATH

As so often happens, most people manage to move on following the huge upheavals in their private lives that a murder investigation and trial may bring.

In the case of John Crabtree, Robert MacCowan, Robert Roberts and the Stocks, they come alive for a brief time as a footnote in books, and then disappear back into obscurity. For others their lives continue to be the focus for historians.

Arthur Newton was able to deliver many more famous briefs to Marshall Hall, but then represented Dr Hawley Harvey Crippen in 1910. One last co-incidence is that Crippen's mistress Ethel le Neve lived in Goldington Buildngs, one of the first council tenants in this new block of flats. The building in Crowndale Road is just around the corner from Mornington Crescent Underground Station, and close to where Walter Sickert was living at the time of the murder.

Crippen's wife Cora often appeared on the stage of the Old Bedford Music Hall, a favourite subject of Sickert.

This was a disastrous time for Newton. He was accused of unprofessional conduct for supposedly passing on a letter from Crippen to the editor of *John Bull*, a scurrilous publication. He was suspended for a year, and in this time joined up with others to perpetrate a fraud which landed him with a three year transportation order to Australia, and to be struck off the Rolls of Solicitors.

Judge Grantham continued to sit on the bench and follow his mildly eccentric lifestyle. He would sometimes appear at the Inns of Court dinners in the scarlet coat, which had descended to him from an ancestor, of the old Bloomsbury Association or 'Devils Own'.

According to David Grantham, his great grandson, he named one of his cottages Bye-Law Cottage, after the local council took him to court over some building regulations that weren't adhered to! He caught pneumonia and died at his house in Eaton Square on 30 November 1911.

Marshall Hall's career continued its meteoric rise. He became Britain's leading criminal defence lawyer and died on 23rd February 1926.

Ruby Young never returned to her home at 13, Finborough Road. She changed her name and fled the country.

Bert Shaw moved away and shortly afterwards married and lived in Manchester. When his wife died he moved in with his sister Ivy in Poole, Dorset. Friends of the family recall him as smartly dressed with rings and silverware, always taking great pride in his appearance. Bert died in the mid 1960s.

I hope this book helps to give comfort to at least one person, Bert's sister Ivy. She wrote to her nephew Robert: 'I feel I had to write to you Bob, I suppose it is a bit of a muddle, but felt for years I would like it made clear that Bert could not have done such a deed. Sorry to have bothered you Robert, but feel easier now.'

Ever since Alan Stanley first contacted me, I have hoped that someone from the Dimmock family may have made contact. So far, there had been no knowledge of to where the family dispersed. No more was heard of William Dimmock after he wrote to the newspaper saying that he was now living in Wellingborough. Of the rest of the family, Rosa, Maud, and Henry there is no trace.

Of Robert Wood there was no more heard of him. Marjoribanks tells a very interesting story. Many years after the trial Marshall Hall was leaving a provincial assize court when a small, happy looking man came up to him.

'You don't know me', said the man.

'No', replied Hall, 'you must forgive me. Wait a moment isn't your name Wood?'

'No', replied the other, 'it's not but I'd like you to know that I am doing very well, and I owe it all to you.'

This has remained Robert Wood's postscript. Then in August 2005, Michael Cotgrove, whom I have mentioned earlier wrote to me stating that: 'I am in close contact with someone who knew Robert Wood very well, albeit in the later stages of his life. Robert Wood did have a wife and two sons and never changed his name.' (Marjoribanks, who is often quoted, claimed that Wood did change his name.)

And Emily. She was buried in Finchley where she first entered service at the age of 16.

The *Daily Mail* published an account of the trial by Sir Hall Caine. I believe the best way to conclude this story of Emily's life is by quoting his words;

'Her dead body was there, indeed, with all the horror of its blood upon it, and the crime committed upon her we were always conscious of, but the woman herself seemed never for a moment to be present to our minds. That poor outcast of the streets, who was no vampire, no alluring temptress lying in wait to wreck the lives of men, but only an outcast girl, very poor, perhaps very worthless, though dowered with a little fatal beauty ... that poor crushed thing, whose existence as the victim of man's lust and the world's grinding poverty had been the prologue to the tremendous drama I had just seem.'

9 POSTSCRIPT

Speech given to the Whitechapel Society on Saturday February 2nd 2008 at the Aldgate Exchange, 133 — 137 Whitechapel High Street, London, E1.

The Whitechapel Society promotes the study of the Whitechapel murders of 1888 and the social impact that this event had on the East End of London.

Although this summarises some of what has been written in previous chapters it also contains previously unpublished material and personal recollections which the reader may find of interest.

Good evening Ladies and Gentlemen. Thank you for inviting me. I thought I'd begin by saying a little bit about myself. My real job is Town Centre Manager in Hertford although before then I managed to scrape a living by writing for magazines and then the author of *The Camden Town Murder*.

I grew up in Camden Town. I was actually born in St Marys Hospital, Paddington and then spent the next 30 years in Rochester Square which backs on to Camden Square. At the back of the garden was the house in which Alan Sillitoe lived for a while and wrote *Gog* in which he mentions Camden Town.

My father was born at the turn of the twentieth century in Hoxton. There is no polite way of saying this but the housing there was by any standards slum dwellings. He took me down once a month to see my grandmother and my mad aunt Polly who was a regular visitor in her later years to the Rochester Square Spiritualist Temple.

They lived in Shepherdess Walk which you may be aware is not so far from here. Now it's been rebuilt and gentrified and possibly a fashionable address but in the early 1950s it was not much different from Whitechapel of 1888.

My father's family was large but a happy one but writing these notes the only colour that comes to mind is black. Everything was black, tall buildings that were grey and grimy, small backstreet businesses that were always dark and shadowy. It's easy even now to imagine the gloom of late Victorian working class housing.

My mother on the other hand was born in Chiswick and her family moved to Rochester Square on the other side from where I was brought up. My grandfather was an ostler and looked after Gilbey's shire horses which were the star turn of the Easter Monday parade in the Inner Circle of Regents Park.

My mother worked at Gilbeys in their Park Royal distillery whilst still carrying me which is where she tells me I obtained my liking for gin. Her sister, my aunt Maud also worked there and on her death I asked for her Gilbeys drinks tray. Around the tray is featured every sign of the zodiac and their preferred drink. For Libra it reads: 'the morning is not your best period, your first drink of the day is most probably an Alka Seltzer.' So you are very fortunate that we are meeting in the evening.

My parents married in 1940 and set up home at No 10 Agar Grove, almost opposite to 29 St Pauls Road as it was then called and where Emily Dimmock met her death.

My father was offered the property to buy but it was during the war and he wasn't going to take the risk. He was quite right. Agar Grove was bombed out. On the site of No 10 there is now a high rise block but No 29 escaped.

It was a popular target for enemy action as the main line railway from Kings Cross ran directly underneath Agar Grove and still does to this day. If you travel into Kings Cross you can see the high-rise block, built on the River Fleet which all the locals knew; but only much later did the builders realise, was sinking at the rate of about one eighth of an inch per year.

I mention this because the railway plays such a big part in this story. Emily's common law husband worked on the railway, their landlady's husband did so as did many of the men interviewed by the police following the murder.

People in those days lived close to their place of work. A short walk away, about ten minutes downhill is Kings Cross station, St Pancras and a short walk further on, Euston. It was not unusual to find men out and about in the hours around dawn on their way to work.

Where you find the railway, you find travellers and there you will find the gasometers and the dark alleyways and arches under the railway bridges no different from that portrayed in Eastenders; and of course the working girls. Just down from Agar Grove is Goods Way, the red light district. It isn't any more because the Eurostar terminal has been built over it. My next door neighbour delivered the sand and building materials and he tells me that the working girls have now moved on to Crowndale Road. But this was Emily Dimmock's world and the area in which she found her clients.

And to the murder of Emily Dimmock. A young girl of twenty-two, living in rented rooms with her common law husband was found with her throat cut on his return from his work on the night shift. It isn't really Camden Town either – St Pauls Road, Agar Grove now, is more a suburb of Kings Cross being close to York Way, a major trunk road north.

So why did the murder of an ordinary young girl, working nights as a prostitute become so famous and become known for the last 100 years as the Camden Town Murder?

It's a question I've been asked so many times over the last four years and never really gave a satisfactory answer.

Emily Dimmock who preferred to be known as

Phyllis was living at 29 St Pauls Road with her common law husband Bert Shaw. She was twenty-two, he was nineteen; born in 1888 – as someone once said, a significant year.

Sir David Napley in his own part fact/part fiction account of the Camden Town Murder claims that they met at St Pancras Station. It could be true but by early 1907 they were living together and had moved addresses quite a few times finally renting rooms from Mrs Stocks.

In those days anyone under the age of twenty-one required their parents consent to marriage. The Shaw family had given that consent and Mrs Shaw had made arrangements to meet her future daughter-in-law and travelled down to London on Thursday 12th September.

Bert was born in Northampton and his family were proud that he had worked his way up to the position of cook on the Midland railway on the London to Sheffield run. As usual he left at 3.30pm on Wednesday 11th September to work on the 4.00pm train.

When Mrs Shaw arrived at Euston, Emily was not there to greet her. She enquired of a police constable who gave her directions to St Pauls Road. She arrived at about 11.00am and was let in by Mrs Stocks and waited outside Emily's rooms which were on the same level as the front door accessed up a flight of stone steps.

I returned to Agar Grove early last year with a film

crew who were filming a documentary for an upcoming series on the Edwardians on BBC4. As we talked at the foot of those same steps a young girl passed us, walked up the steps and a few moments later the light in what would have been Emily's front room was turned on and the shutters closed. The light was fading and we were discussing Emily's habit of drinking in the Eagle pub in Royal College Street – a five minute walk away - when the girl arrived. It was very eerie; no one said a word, as if she was a spirit from the past walking through us.

When the producer of that film Waldemar Januszczack wrote an article in *The Sunday Times* about the Walter Sickert exhibition he referred to me as 'a marvellous local character; a London geezer of the old school who had an extraordinary resemblance to Arthur Mullard.' I am still unsure as to whether it was meant as a compliment

Mrs Shaw waited for Bert's return at about 11.30am. He had no keys so Mrs Stocks let them in. To his horror Bert found Emily on their bed in the back room as if fast asleep but her throat had been cut almost to the point where her head had been severed.

Inspector Neil from Kentish Town police station was called and then the Police Surgeon who later confirmed that Emily had been killed between 3.00am and 5.00am on the morning of 12th September.

As Neil went about his investigation Emily's double

life soon became public. All her previous clients were tracked down and all had strong alibis. But the description of one man kept recurring. A man of medium height, with a blue serge suit and bowler hat who had a distinctive walk and who Emily had known for some time.

A man seeking work in nearby Brewery Road told the investigation that he had seen a man fitting that description leaving 29 St Pauls Road at 5.30am that morning. A young artists model - to use her expression by the name of Ruby Young recognised the description and the handwriting on a postcard found in Emily's possession which was copied in the *News of the World*.

This was the famous 'Rising Sun' postcard addressed to Mrs B Shaw saying ' Phillis Darling. If it pleases you meet me at 8.15pm at the, and here the writer had inserted a handdrawn picture of a rising sun. Yours to a cinder, Alice.' The Rising Sun was one of Emily's favourite haunts in the Euston Road.

The postcard was only found when Bert Shaw was leaving St Pauls Road and clearing out their belongings. Emily had collected postcards and the murderer appeared to have ransacked her room and collections as if looking for one in particular. It had been hidden under the lining of a drawer.

Ruby Young led the police to Grays Inn Road and pointed out Robert Charles Thomas Cavers Wood, a twenty-nine years old graphic artist. Wood was arrested, charged and tried for murder in December 1907.

It has been accepted that the man who was to become England's premier criminal defence lawyer Edward Marshall Hall conducted a brilliant defence, and following what was considered a slightly bizarre summing up by Judge Grantham, Robert Wood was acquitted after only eighteen minutes deliberation by the jury. The case was closed and the murderer has never been found.

So who did murder Emily Dimmock?

I believe nothing more might have happened but for a series of events in 2002. By 2001 my mother had slipped into the early stages of dementia and in order to help her memory I wrote an article for *Stage* magazine on the Old Bedford Music Hall. The Bedford had stood in Camden High Street since 1861 and despite being destroyed by fire was rebuilt in 1899 and she and my father often went there. All the great music hall stars played there – Gracie Fields, Marie Lloyd, George Robey amongst others. As with a lot of my other articles I put this on my website including about two lines on artist Walter Sickert of whom I had never heard, as he had lived close by in Mornington Crescent and painted scenes of the theatre.

Along with many other music halls the Bedford fell victim to Hollywood and during the Second World War was bombed and remained derelict for many years. Then it fell into terminal decay – it did not stop my mother from asking bus conductors to put her off at the Bedford.

On the other side of the Atlantic, Patricia Cornwell had just published *Portrait of a Killer* and had put Walter Sickert firmly in the frame as Jack the Ripper and despite a nineteen years gap a clear candidate for the Camden Town Murder as well.

At about the same time in Northampton a man called Alan Stanley was researching his family tree. He had looked up Camden Town and found a few articles by myself and emailed me: 'You seem to know a lot about Camden Town what do you know about the Camden Town Murder?'

'Absolutely nothing' I replied.

So began four years of research. Alan and I became good friends by phone and email. We met only once when he came to Hertford to drop off his daughter at the University in Hatfield. We agreed to meet at the Salisbury Arms Hotel and despite not having met previously we approached the hotel from opposite ends of Fore Street and recognised each other immediately.

Alan's interest in the story was that Bert Shaw was his great uncle. There was always a cloud hanging over the family whilst his complete innocence continued to be doubted and no one else had been convicted.

Alan sent me a copy of a photograph taken of Bert

Shaw in his later years whilst living with his sister in Poole. Despite many requests I have respected his wishes and this has never been released into the public domain. It shows Bert playing cards in Ivy's living room; slightly balding, a little portly but a well dressed, healthy man with a waistcoat and watch chain.

Bert was the first suspect but he had a cast iron alibi – he was in Derby. The family are quite sure of this although many accounts give his overnight stay as being in Sheffield.

I never had much cause to doubt this but posts on the Casebook website have raised the possibility that he could have made two journeys and had time to return home, murder Emily and still arrive home as usual at 11.30am. I don't know if this was ever proven as being possible but would have needed a good copy of *Bradshaw's Railway Timetable*s to get the timings right.

I signed a copy of my book for John Workman our local fishmonger who told me he had a deep interest in murder mysteries. John the Fish told me that it was quite common amongst shift workers such as Bert for a fellow worker to replace another and sign a colleague on for a shift if the other wanted a night off.

I don't know how this could ever be checked but just when you think you've got the case straight someone comes along and rains on your parade.

So what would have been Bert's motive? As we know they were due to get married and with his parents consent. They had been living together for some time although had moved around the area quite a bit.

On Emily's death particulars of their private life became known. She was born in Little Hadham a small village in Hertfordshire. Her father William ran a beer house called the Red Lion. At the age of eleven they were living in Hitchin where she was seriously injured by a runaway horse. At sixteen, Emily was working as a maid at the Swan Hotel, Bedford and although she spent brief periods at home it was not long after, that under the influence of a friend she found herself in London.

Here she moved around from address to address in the Kings Cross/Euston area, apparently earning a living as a prostitute. During this time she met and was friends with Robert Wood.

Around the same time, she had met Bert Shaw with whom she set up home. On her death it became clear that they were living way beyond their means. Bert was earning about a guinea a week on the trains but nearly all their possessions were being bought on credit. They had a piano and a sewing machine listed amongst things repossessed. Emily had a talent for both sewing and music but not the means to pay for it.

So it would appear that Bert gave more than a nod towards Emily's nocturnal activities. And as such they were not much different from many other Edwardian couples. St Pauls Road was and still is a desirable area of residence and as couples tried to raise themselves above the poverty of working class drudgery they borrowed money – but it had to be paid back, so Emily worked at night. In *Partridges Dictionary of the Underworld* Emily might have been known as an 'enthusiastic amateur'.

But as debts mounted the couple started to move around lodgings to escape the tally man. Hence the famous music hall song – 'My old man said follow the van'. What my parents would call a moonlight flit. So around this time you had a very mobile population, escaping debt by whatever means and I believe one of the reasons why Walter Sickert's titles of his canvasses reflected this sub-culture. The Camden Town Murder becomes 'What shall we do about the rent?'

Bert Shaw may have been overcome by jealousy but it seems unlikely, as they had settled into an accepted lifestyle.

So if not Bert then who else? Well it seems there were no lack of suspects as Inspector Neil tracked down many of her previous clients – nearly all of whom had a form of employment connected to the railway. Most of them had contracted venereal disease and were quite sure that they had been infected by Emily. Strangely, the Police Surgeon was able to confirm that although there was evidence of having had syphilis she was clear at the time of her death.

As I have said, suspicion began to fall around the

stranger with the blue serge suit and odd walk. I started to look at Edwardian photos. Nearly every middle class office based male owned a bowler hat and wore a blue serge suit – it was a popular material although having a one slight defect as the song says – 'like the shine on his blue serge suit'. A contemporary photograph of a Cup Final football crowd is remarkable for the fact that every spectator is wearing a hat.

Ruby Young was able to identify Robert Wood and he was brought to trial. Despite his respectable background and artistic occupation Robert Wood was a consummate liar.

He lied about not ever having known Emily but witness after witness testified to seeing her in his company over the previous two years, and at least one to the fact that at one time they had shared lodgings. He lied about not having seen Emily on the night she died, as both a friend and the barmaid testified to him being there with Emily in the Eagle pub, and leaving with her at about 9.30pm. It made a nonsense of his alibi which was that he was in the habit of seeing Ruby Young on a Wednesday night although they had parted months earlier.

Of one thing he was able to be certain that he arrived home in Grays Inn Road at about midnight as there were witnesses to prove that.

It remained to be discovered who was the man seen

leaving 29 St Pauls Road at about 5.30am on the morning of 12th September.

Edward Marshall Hall's career had taken a nosedive and it was a brave man that took on the defence of Robert Wood but Hall needed any brief he could get.

His team tracked down a railway worker who was also a part-time boxer and confirmed that he had passed Emily's lodging at about 5.30am on his way to work and owing to his boxing training had a certain swing to his walk.

Hall then convinced the jury that although Wood had lied he had done so to protect his family from the public humiliation of his being with a known prostitute. But as the Police Surgeon had confirmed death as between 3.00am and 5.00am, Wood was already home and had an alibi.

Robert Wood was acquitted and owed his life to Marshall Hall. The case became famous and up until now I have only ever made some weak assumptions as to why. I believe there are at least two main reasons.

First the manner in which Robert Wood was identified. It would not be out of place in a plotline for new tricks as I'm not so sure that police procedure now allows for witnesses to be escorted by the investigating team to a suspect's place of work to be identified at a safe distance.

It backfired on poor Ruby who was hounded out of court in disguise to the shouts of the crowd who called her 'Judas' and 'Won't you come out tonight Ruby'. It was Wood who had lied about seeing her. She had told the truth.

Secondly a vital piece of police evidence: the famous postcard was photocopied and placed in every newspaper including the *News of the World*, which is where Ruby recognised it and the writing. Which is how a very ordinary murder in a very ordinary suburb of North London became known around the country.

And as a result all the elements of Edwardian life came to court. The judge and barristers were from the privileged classes and West End clubs, the jury from the respectable ranks of shopkeepers, property owners and professional people. Jury service was far from being universal; only the property owner or head of the household was eligible for service, certainly no women and as has been seen the working classes were so mobile for reasons of debt that they were not going to have their addresses recorded for officialdom to track them down.

I soon discovered that the Discovery Channel made the Camden Town Murder the third most popular murder mystery after Jack the Ripper and the Peasenhall Murder.

Robert Wood was acquitted and the real culprit never found. Then two events occurred. In her quest for supporting evidence Patricia Cornwell came upon the Camden Town Murder even though it was 19 years after the last canonical Ripper murder. She decided that Walter Sickert may have done this one as well without much evidence to support that claim either.

The one factor that counts against the Ripper theory is that Emily was not mutilated. Her throat was cut with a single stroke of a sharp blade. She was in the position of sleep with no defensive cuts. Slitting someone's throat is not a simple task unless the victim is taken from behind or by complete surprise; otherwise they have time to defend themselves. Just this week my son who works in Social Care Provision told me of a client that had committed suicide by cutting his own throat in a manner similar to Emily.

Fortunately for me, Ms Cornwell's book brought the Camden Town Murder back into the public interest and to the attention of Alan Stanley. From this I started to research the case and as it developed put it on my website. Other people doing searches on Google did the rest.

One of the people to contact me was Paul Brooks. You may be familiar with him as a Ripper author and a published work, *By Ear and Eyes*. Paul had looked at the Camden Town Murder, and had included Walter Sickert, because Patricia Cornwell had brought the issue to our attention.

He kindly sourced the file from the Public Records Office – over a thousand pages of it and sent on to me any relevant bits I needed. Paul's greatest contribution was to examine the Police Surgeon's evidence and with his own specialist knowledge as a forensic pathologist placed the time of death as much earlier than 3.00am on the 12th September.

His conclusion was that death could have occurred at any time after 10.30pm on the night of 11th September – as one of my friends has said another interesting date. This would have placed Robert Wood back at the scene of the crime; his alibi had already been found to be a fabrication of lies and he had been seen with Emily only an hour earlier.

Both prosecuting and defence counsel were happy with the official time of death. The prosecution had a witness who could say that they saw a man fitting Wood's description leaving at the right time and the defence case was that Robert Wood was already at home.

But Wood had given a false alibi, and only he knew where he was between the hours of 9.30pm and midnight on the night of 11th September. He had opportunity and as much motive in the form of jealousy as Bert Shaw.

Modern forensic science may have placed a suspect more definitely at the scene of crime but in 1907 it was not so advanced. Perhaps the murderer will never be found. I began this book accepting the long held belief of Wood's innocence, but in his summing up at the end of case Inspector Neil expresses his view that there was no one else who could have done it.

If not Bert Shaw then who else – the only name is that of Robert Wood for the previous reasons. There is little other contemporary evidence and despite the best efforts none of us have been able to track down living relatives of either the Dimmocks or the Woods.

Then almost as the book was going to print I received a very angry email from a close friend of one of Robert Wood's family. Apart from a few factual errors about age and names they had little else to add apart from the fact that despite the stories that Robert Wood had changed his name and moved away, he had in fact not changed his name, had remained in London and led an interesting career as a graphic artist. He had children and passed away at a good age.

I offered to add a postscript; even that they could write one themselves to balance what I had said. The family and the family friend disappeared as quickly as they had appeared only reminding me what a caring, kind and sensitive man Robert Wood was.

About a few months later I received another email from a lady saying that she was Robert Wood's granddaughter and had not known of this case until contacted by the family friend above of whom she only had a bare knowledge. The latter had obviously given her own version so I replied at length explaining how I had reached my conclusions and nothing more was heard from there either.

After so long, more than 100 years it is a little irritating not to close the case. Alan Stanley has passed on much of our work to the family although many close to Bert have now also passed away. I have said elsewhere that I hope my conclusions help to give those remaining a little peace but you can never be certain.

There I will have to leave it unless someone else comes along to prove me wrong. It is sad that Emily's death has led to my own fortune. Not so much monetary as I haven't received any royalties yet but I've enjoyed a good run over the last few years.

I have been featured in local papers and media, been interviewed for a radio show by a Dutch graduate for his PhD and appeared in a documentary. I've sold a lot of books locally and signed them but the first copy that I ever signed was at the request of Loretta Lay for one of her customers – Jeremy Beadle. I remain very flattered.

So yes it's been a good run and to remind you where I began a few hours ago my Gilbeys drinks horoscope tray concludes with these words: 'You display a great ability to obtain a drink at any time of day or night'. Thank you.

This ended my presentation.

You may wonder at the reference to Jeremy Beadle.

He was not just a famous television presenter, he raised millions for charity and was a respected authority on Jack the Ripper and regularly attended meetings of the Whitechapel Society. At the meeting of 2nd February a tape was played of Jeremy hosting the Christmas quiz in 2007. Jeremy Beadle passed away on 30 January 2008.

At the conclusion of my presentation I was happy to answer questions. I had brought a copy of Emily's death certificate for members to see and more than one asked why it carried a note from the Coroner stating that she had been murdered by Robert Wood before the trial had even commenced. A member of the audience confirmed that at that time a coroner had these powers if enough evidence had been produced to justify such a statement.

The relative of Robert Wood who had contacted me through an intermediary then wrote to me with a copy of Emily's death certificate which had been amended. After the cause of death and notation of Robert Wood's guilt had been added the clause 'tried and acquitted'. This had been a long and exhaustive process and I acknowledge that lady's effort and resolve.

Some discussion has already taken place of the word – 'synapse'. This has now been clarified, as from the trial summary which is contained in the final chapter, Doctor Thompson stated that death was from 'syncope arising from a sudden loss of blood.' In other words unconsciousness, quickly followed by death arising from a lack of oxygen to the brain.

The Emily Dimmock's Death Certificate showing the amendment.

10 THE FINAL WORD

Conclusions from the Trial Summary

Following the digitalisation and publication in April 2008 of all trials at the Old Bailey from 1674 to 1913 the summary of the trial of Robert Wood is now available. This has helped to clear some outstanding issues and enable a more reasoned conclusion to the case.

The first thing to put to rest is the possibility that Bert Shaw could have murdered Emily Dimmock. His position in the Midland Railway was of 'dining car attendant'. Although the family believed him to be in Derby he testified to being in Sheffield and this could be confirmed by a fellow employee who was sleeping in a house opposite. When pressed even Marshall Hall did not wish to pursue this line of enquiry.

Bert Shaw who we must remember was only nineteen at this time said he gave Emily £1.00 per week for housekeeping out of which he believed that she paid the landlady Mrs Stocks 6 shillings. Sarah Stocks claimed that the rent was 8 shillings.

Over the three overnight stays between 9th and 11th September the ships' cook Roberts (named here as Thomas Percival Roberts – not Robert) claimed he had left 42 shillings as payment to Emily for services rendered. This was 2 guineas (there being 20 shillings to the pound and a guinea being £1. 1shilling in pre-decimal currency), almost as much as Bert would earn in two weeks. This was a lot of money and none of it was recovered by Bert.

Along with this cash Bert claimed that the house keys, Emily's rings of which one was a wedding ring to give people the impression of marriage, a couple of chains, 5 shillings in cash, a silver watch and a cigarette case with the initials 'W.A.S.' were all missing.

On the afternoon of 11th September everything was as normal. Bert left about 4.30pm and Emily was engaged in laundry dressed in a brown velvet skirt and a light blouse. The next time Emily was seen was by Mr Stocks who saw her leave 29 St Pauls Road at about 8.30pm dressed in a green costume with her hair still in metal curling pins.

Emily was last seen alive that evening for about an hour from 9.00pm in the Eagle public house in Great (now Royal) College Street both by the barmaid Lily Raven and Joseph Lambert a friend of Robert Wood with whom she had entered.

When Bert Shaw arrived home he had only the latch key to let himself in through the front door. The doors of the front parlour and the back bedroom which both opened onto the passageway; and the dividing doors in their room were all locked and the keys were missing. It was Emily's habit to leave these doors unlocked for when Bert returned.

Doctor John Thompson, Divisional Surgeon arrived at about 1.00pm and stated that Emily was cold and although difficult to assess exactly how long rigor mortis had set in, stated that it was certainly quite a few hours. Following a Post Mortem he was also able to confirm that Emily had taken of a meal about 3 hours before death as there were traces of potatoes, bread and mint sauce in her stomach. He added that both of these means of determining time of death were not precise and could be influenced by many other factors.

In his own testimony Detective Inspector Neil confirmed that he had found the remains of a meal on the table; possibly a lamb shank and a cup of mint sauce nearby. Emily's stomach showed she had consumed a dark liquid, and a half bottle of stout and empty glass were found on the table.

I have mentioned before, that in 1907 forensic science was in its infancy, but Inspector Neil testified that there were no fingerprints found on the tumblers in Emily's room.

On the basis of this evidence, Thompson estimated time of death to be between 4.00am and 5.30am, on the morning of 12th September.

He testified that Emily had once contracted syphilis but was not infected at that time and after several microscopic examinations could find no evidence of any semen or recent sexual activity. Bert Shaw testified that he had never known Emily sleep nude.

Although the contents of the stomach and the intestinal tract are but one guide to the time of death there is no way of knowing whether Emily ate a meal of lamb and potatoes - a light meal which takes less time to be digested - before she left 29 St Pauls Road at 8.30pm or if it was consumed on her return.

A meal taken at about 8.00pm – 8.30pm would give an approximate time of death at about 11.00pm – 11.30pm. Thompson estimated that because of the contents of the stomach the digestive process had been going on for about three to four hours. There are no reasons given why Thompson assumed that Emily ate supper very late. Supper time is a loose term and usually a meal taken a few hours before bed so as not to disturb a good night's sleep with indigestion. It is usually a cold meal, perhaps from the remains of dinner. There were plates with an amount of cutlery left for washing, possibly from an earlier meal, found by Inspector Neil.

Roberts made no reference to eating at 29 St Pauls Road whilst in Emily's company and on all three nights they had left the Rising Sun quite late, usually past midnight. These were the days before the events of the

First World War and the Defence of the Realm Act which restricted the time that working men were allowed to drink in pubs. It took another 80 years before licensing restrictions were loosened in England.

Despite his attempts at fabricating an alibi it was determined from the evidence of Lily Raven and Joseph Lambert that Robert Wood was with Emily Dimmock from about 9.00pm on the night of 11th September.

In her evidence Lily Raven states that they left together at about 10.00pm. In his own evidence Robert Wood disputed this by saying that he and Emily remained in the passageway of the pub until 11.00pm after which only he left to go home, leaving Emily in the bar.

After testimony by Emily's brother for purposes of identification the next person to testify at the trial was Detective Alfred Gros (?). He had measured distances between the various houses mentioned in the investigation and stated that the distance between 29 St Pauls Road and 12 Frederick Street, the home of Robert Wood, was one and a half miles. There is little difference in the distance from the Eagle but in all three cases from St Pauls Road by way of York Way, Midland Road or Great College Street the journey is downhill. Therefore the walk would take about 30 minutes, considerably less if in a hurry.

Robert Wood stated that he arrived home between

half past eleven and twelve. His half brother James normally arrived home between 11.00pm and midnight; on the night of September 11th George Wood, Robert's father recalls James coming home at about 11.30pm.

James and his father shared a room; Robert occupied the room next door. When he arrived home he took the clock that was in the shared room to his own room. His father places the time that night at about midnight. The doors in both rooms opened into the passageway.

The lodger on the floor above them, a Mr Joseph Rogers, was in the garden digging for worms – he was looking forward to a fishing competition that weekend – and recalls Robert Wood coming home between 11.30pm and 11.40pm. There is nothing to clarify how he could have been so accurate as there is no mention of any timepiece being in his possession.

All this evidence places Robert Wood at home by midnight on the evening of September 11th. Although there is no reason to dispute the testimony of the witnesses, the veracity of that time slot can be substantiated by Wood's ex-lover Ruby Young.

We know that Wood had asked her to provide a false alibi by admitting that he continued to spend Mondays and Wednesdays with her. He had given her a story with which to tell anyone who asked about their movements on that night that they had separated at Hyde Park Corner at about 10.30; and he had come back by tube to King's Cross getting home about midnight.

Therefore Robert Wood was looking to cover his movements for the last few hours of September 11th. He had said to Ruby that he had met Emily on the Monday and needed her to cover for him for that night. On the Wednesday he was out walking alone, and as he had no one to prove where he was he asked her to say that she was with him then also. Ruby asked him where he was on that Wednesday; *'but he gave me no answer; he said he could not prove it.'*

As both his father and stepbrother were certain that he had not left the house again until the next morning, and Doctor Thompson had placed time of death at about 5.00am on the morning of 12th September, this would have put Wood in the clear and have made sense of Marshall Hall's defence that the gaining of a false alibi was no more that to shield family from the knowledge that he had been mixing with prostitutes. Or even just to deny any contact with Emily on the night of her death.

Whatever the reason it was accepted.

However, if Lily Raven is to be believed and Emily and Robert Wood left the Eagle together at about 10.00pm then there is a period of about two hours for which Wood has no alibi at all.

29 St Pauls Road was a busy house. There were many lodgers and one of the earliest risers was the

landlord George Stocks. He usually left for work at about 5.30am and his alarm was set for 4.40am. Anyone moving about on the floor above could have been heard by him. The ship's cook Roberts testified that he left Emily in the mornings at about 7.30am, probably on the nod of Emily who was aware of the comings and goings of the household and knew the best time for a client to slip out with the best chance of being undetected.

The Shaw's accommodation consisted of two rooms both of which had doors leading into the passageway. There was a set of dividing doors between the two rooms which could be locked. As we know all three doors had been locked and the keys never found.

When Inspector Neil first interviewed Robert Wood at his home in 12 Frederick Street, he noted that the arrangement between George Wood, his stepson James and Robert Wood was exactly the same as that at 29 St Pauls Road, except that the dividing doors were blocked on both sides by furniture. It would appear that Robert Wood might have felt very much at home in St Pauls Road.

I have commented before that cutting someone's throat is not an easy means of murder unless the victim is either unconscious or taken completely unaware. Although Emily's throat had been cut to the point where her head was almost severed she was found in the position of sleep, her head resting on the bed.

This, as Thompson testified would have accounted for the lack of blood spattered patterns on the wall, and if the assailant had used a handkerchief or similar cloth to cover their hands there would have been a minimum of blood on their person.

I formed an opinion as to how she had been attacked. I should say that the assailant was at her back on the bed between her and the wall. The head must have been slightly raised either by placing the hand under the forehead or by grasping the hair — more likely I should say by placing the hand on the forehead, raised sufficiently to get the sharp instrument as far back as possible to the throat. The head at first evidently was not raised sufficiently for the instrument to pass between the head and the bed. Consequently, there was a clean cut on the sheet and the tick of the bed. When a sufficient height had been obtained, it was simply a matter of a moment. There need not have been much blood necessarily on the assailant except upon the right hand.

The assailant would not necessarily have to get over the body to get out of the bed onto the floor. He might have got out at the foot of the bed. When an artery is severed there is an enormous spurt of blood, but in this case the neck was towards the bed and the blood would spurt into the bed. If the wound was inflicted with a

*razor the razor must have been held in a firm grip, or a
handkerchief might have been tied round the tang to
keep the blade in position and hold it rigid. The razor,
or whatever instrument was employed, would be simply
swamped in blood, and it would be difficult to get the
blood out of the interstices between the blade and the
handle of the razor. Under these circumstances I
believe it would be difficult. I came to the conclusion for
that reason that neither of the razors belonging to the
prisoner had been used.'*

The murder weapon was never found; it may have
been one of Bert Shaw's razors which the murderer
took away with him and disposed of later. We will
never know; but of Robert Wood?

If Lily Raven is to be believed, and he and Emily left
the Eagle at about 10.00pm, then he had the time to
commit this crime and return home by midnight,
which is the time for which he asked Ruby for an alibi;
not 5.00am which Thompson had set. One and a half
miles is not a long walk downhill for a man in a state of
panic and desperate to get away.

Whoever it was had an understanding of the layout
of St Pauls Road and took the keys with them. There
would not have been much blood on the attacker either
and there was evidence in the wash bowl and petticoat
that the attacker had made an attempt to clean away the
blood.

As Robert Wood admitted to Ruby Young, he had no way of proving where he was on the night of September 11th. No one came forward to confirm the time he left the Eagle so it is one person's word against another's. There must always be an element of doubt; and that most probably saved Robert Wood from the gallows.

And the question that has been asked before: if not Robert Wood then who else?

Enter John William Crabtree; horse-thief, brothel-keeper and self-confessed teetotaller. He had been one of the many people who had known Robert Wood over a period of two years or more and was aware of his relationship with Emily. He was called before an identification parade although he was none too fond of the police and proved to be obstructive; whether deliberately or otherwise is open to debate.

Crabtree leased 1 Bidborough Street and this was one of the addresses at which Emily lodged and where Robert Wood had been seen with her as a regular visitor.

Amongst other men who came looking for Emily was a man that Crabtree only knew as 'Scottie'. Even Crabtree who was no stranger to the seedier side of life was in awe of this man. Scottie had threatened Emily on more than one occasion. Emily had handed over money to him and whilst she was in Portsmouth with the sailor Henry Biddle, Scottie had come to Bidborough Street to find her.

This is Crabtree's witness statement: *'the man I have described called at the house, and, finding she was gone, got very angry, swore about her, and threatened to do for her. He wanted to go to her room, and when I would not let him he got a razor and opened it, took his handkerchief from his pocket, wrapped it round the handle of the razor, and, waving it, said he would do her in yet.'*

Compare this with the murder method and the way of holding a razor as described by Thompson. I doubt if Thompson and Crabtree moved in the same circles but the similarity is startling.

When he heard of Emily's murder Crabtree's first thought was that the culprit was Scottie and when called to an identification parade on October 5th had expected to pick out Scottie from the fifteen men present.

He refused to identify Robert Wood: *'There is a man here who knew Phyllis Dimmock but the man that I have referred to in my statement is not here. I came here to identify another man and I shan't pick this man out.'*

Eventually at the insistence of Inspector Neil he picked out Wood as being the friend of the deceased.

The identity of Scottie was never established. It was ascertained though that 'Scotch Bob' whose real name was Alexander Mackie was not Scottie and he was in Glasgow on the night of the murder. Crabtree appears to have had some association with Scottie as he claimed that he saw him about two weeks earlier (than the trial date) and that Scottie had accused him of informing on him to the police and 'putting a halter around his neck' – an underworld slang term for the hangman's noose.

There were two other strange sightings of Emily which have never been easily explained.

Witnesses stated that they saw her in the company of a man in the Somers Town area of Kings Cross between 2.00pm and 4.00pm on the 11th despite Bert Shaw stating on oath that *'deceased had not been out that day'*, and the Stocks sure that she had not left the house until after 8.30pm on the evening of 11th September to post a letter to her sister, which was also later verified.

This was in Inspector Neil's report of 30th September in which he refers to three statements by a Mr Clarke of Seymour Street, Gladys Bucknal (?) and Mrs Walton of St Pancras Square where Emily had once lodged. There is no mention of the relationship between these three people and they were not called to court.

They had seen Emily in Seymour Street and Phoenix Street, Somers Town arm in arm with *'a tall fair man dressed in a blue serge suit and bowler hat and of a smart gentlemanly appearance'*.

In the same report Neil mentions the two men Habit (Harold) Sharples and Frederick Harvey. Neither of these were cross examined in court but their witness statements were allowed. They gave their professions as 'commission agent' and 'music vendor' respectively but known to Inspector Neil as pimps.

They claim to have seen Emily at 12.10 in the early morning of 12th September in the company of a *'biggish, well built smartish man with a bowler hat'* who was taller than the one they had seen Emily in the company of in the Rising Sun. By this they meant Robert Wood. The man they recognised had been with Emily on Sunday September 8th but he was a stranger to them and had not been in the pub before.

Despite having come forward voluntarily their evidence was not given much credence by Neil as no one else had seen Emily at that time despite being a regular figure in that vicinity and because of their background.

It was certainly odd that two men of doubtful character living on the edges of criminality would voluntarily come forward with such evidence. Sharples and Harvey were well known in the area, by the staff at the Rising Sun and by Scotch Bob.

Of all Emily's friends interviewed none appeared to have been in the Rising Sun on Sunday September 8th , when Sharples and Harvey state they saw the stranger, later spotted by them in the early hours of 12th September. The only man in Emily's company that night was Roberts, but at 12.10 on September 12th in the company of Frank Clarke, he was being let in to his lodgings by his landlady Amelia La Sage.

Neil remarks that the witness statements regarding the sighting at 4.00pm and 12.10am were similar as to the description of the man seen in Emily's company and did not fit Robert Wood. There is no description of Roberts but as a sailor on leave it is unlikely he would possess a bowler hat, or a blue serge suit.

Was the description given by those witnesses that of Scottie? He has never been given a proper name and only ever referred to by Crabtree by his monicker. Crabtree did not like Scottie and as a landlord had been on the receiving end of his temper. Emily had also lodged at 27 St Pancras Buildings, the address given by two of the other witnesses and I can only surmise that they too might have been at the wrong end of Scottie's temper.

Alexander Mackie known as Scotch Bob was for some time confused with Scottie and admitted that he knew Sharples and Harvey and I presume would have liked to have put some distance between himself and his Scottish namesake. If Crabtree is to be believed then Scottie was convinced that he had been 'put in the frame' for Emily's murder. Perhaps a good time to print Crabtree's own evaluation of his character:

'I think I tell the truth sometimes. I try to. I have lived 56 years and have only been in prison three times. I do

not know that my state of mind has been inquired into.
I am sober; I have never tasted liquor in my life.
As to why the police came to me, that is a question for
them. When they came to me I was frightened out of
my life, because I thought they were coming to me for
the murder; and what they said to me I did not believe
at the time. I did not know when the girl had been
murdered. The police have a certain way of going
about; they do not tell the truth always when seeking
information. They tell lies to get at the truth of things;
that is my experience. I have not made a statement I
cannot substantiate.'

However this is the underworld inhabited by the likes of Crabtree, Sharples and Harvey and in which Emily Dimmock moved freely amongst her many lady friends in the bars of Kings Cross and Camden Town. She had many enemies amongst her male acquaintances, some of whom she had co-habited with for a while, some of whom she had infected with syphilis.

Neil was unwilling to give Sharples and Harvey the benefit of the doubt on the grounds that Emily was such a common figure in those parts she would have been seen by others. Many of the public houses were just closing and there would have been many drinkers on their way home.

I mention this only as a theory that perhaps there was a conspiracy to frame Scottie conceived by Mackie,

Sharples, Harvey and a few others. Scottie was never mentioned by anyone else but Crabtree; but he was sure that he would have seen him when called to participate in the identity parade. As much as Neil would have expected Emily to have been seen in the locality no one saw Scottie that night either.

Sharples and Harvey came forward on the afternoon of the murder and would have been aware that the crime was committed in the early morning of 12th September, many hours after they claimed to have seen Emily with the stranger. It was an odd show of public duty by two men who would normally have preferred to keep in the shadows.

I admit that this is a fanciful theory designed only to fit statements made at the time; even those by characters not known for their shows of truth and honesty.

If Emily had left Wood at the Eagle and ventured into Kings Cross her aim would have been to have found one partner for the night. Thomas Roberts was waiting for her at the Rising Sun. It is possible that she met her killer, possibly the man Sharples and Harvey saw her with, but unlikely that she would have taken him back to her lodgings for a light supper of lamb and potatoes with a glass of stout before falling asleep and then offering up her throat.

Crabtree testified that Wood was a regular visitor to his various houses and usually stayed until morning. On the evenings of September 9th and September 10th both Roberts and Wood were in the Rising Sun and at different times in conversation with Emily as testified by friends of Emily and the brother of the licensee. As we know on three occasions Emily left with Roberts and took him back to her rooms.

This might have been the catalyst for Robert Wood – unremitting jealousy. If Lily Raven's testimony is to be believed Wood had no alibi for the hours between ten and twenty minutes to twelve on the night of 11th September.

I attended the Whitechapel Society meeting on February 2nd with a good friend of mine who has contributed much to this book and we were discussing possible motives. Emily was about to be married and we thought that this provided Wood with at least one classic cause for murder – 'If I cannot have her, then no one can'.

On at least two nights prior to her death, Wood had seen her leave for home with another man, and this must have added to his frustration. As Thompson has said there was no sexual activity between Emily and her killer, so the meeting may have been the basis for sorting things out as happens between people who have had a long but eventful relationship. This too would go some way to explaining the charred letter found in Emily's grate asking her to meet the writer at the Eagle pub at 8.30pm.

Wood admitted to having written letters to Ruby

Young and often wrote to Emily. Crabtree testified that he had many of his letters addressed to Emily in his possession. Wood's handwriting style was known to many people and his work colleagues testified to that fact at the trial, which made identification of the sender of the Rising Sun postcard and charred letter that much easier.

Emily might have met Roberts once more at the Rising Sun on the 11th but for the letter; instead she met Wood at the Eagle.

Lily Raven heard her say to the man she was sitting down with, *'Fancy you making me come out like this.'* To the last Robert Wood tried to convince the jury of his own version of events and in doing so accusing others of making false witness statements:

> *'I think it was after 11 when I left the house. Miss Raven is quite inaccurate when she says about 10. I left Dimmock in the bar of the "Eagle." Raven is wrong in saying we left together. There is a corridor that leads to the door — I believe Dimmock rose from her seat and bade me "Good-bye" in the corridor. I do not remember if Raven served me.'*

"You know," said my friend. "I don't think he set out to kill her that night."

"No, nor do I," I agreed.

But I have to admit now that if anyone had time,

motive and opportunity to murder Emily Dimmock, then all the evidence points to Robert Wood.

SELECT BIBLIOGRAPHY

This is a short list of books that may be of interest:

Great Murder Trials of the Twentieth Century
-The Camden Town Murder
by **Sir David Napley**.

Published in hardback in 1987 by Weidenfeld and Nicholson. This is now out of print but copies can usually be found on Amazon or ebay. As mentioned in my own account this is a largely fictionalised account based on the facts but mostly in the style of a modern TV docudrama. It owes much, as do many other accounts to the next two books.

The Life of Sir Edward Marshall Hall
by **Edward Marjoribanks**.

Originally published in hardback in 1929 by Victor Gollancz and then in paperback by Penguin. An abridged edition also published in 1929 by the same author was titled *Famous Trials of Marshall Hall.*. Both of these are also out of print but like the above can be found on many auction sites; this is how I found my own copy of 'Famous Trials'.

The Ripper File

There are hundreds, possibly thousands of books written on the subject of Jack the Ripper and the Whitechapel murders. I cannot list them all. However these are three that have been referred to:

Portrait of a Killer - Case Closed
by Patricia Cornwell.

Still widely available in both hardback and paperback in most book shops.

Sickert and the Ripper Crimes
by Jean Overton Fuller.

Miss Fuller has told me that she has written a postscript to earlier editions as a result of Ms Cornwell's book and this is now in print. It is in paperback but not widely available. A search on Amazon may be the best route but also it can be ordered direct from her publishers
- Mandrake, PO Box 250, Oxford, OX1 1AP, UK.

The Ripper and the Royals
by Melvyn Fairclough.

This is a recent publication in both hardback and paperback but not always easily available. As above a search through Amazon may be more fruitful.

By Ear and Eyes
by **Karyo Magellan** - Longshot Publishing..
This book on Jack the Ripper also contains a section on the Camden Town Murder.

Paul Brooks' excellent website on a forensic approach to the Ripper killings (but not to the identity) can be found at **www.karyom.com/ W h i t e c h a p e l H O W M A N Y . h t m**

For anyone who wishes to access the file at the Public Record Office at Kew the reference number is: **MEP03/182.**

Index

THE AUTHOR

John Barber at work,
photograph courtesy of
the *Hertfordshire Mercury.*

John Barber is an investigator, researcher and writer with a popular and informative website, www.johnbarber.com featuring excellent articles on the socio-cultural history of Britain and its great metropolis London. His published works also include a murder mystery novel, entitled *A Little Local Affair.*

MANDRAKE
CLASSIC CRIME STUDIES

presents

more
exhaustive investigations
of
true crime cases

that have captured
the public's imagination

EXHUMATION OF A MURDER
THE LIFE AND TRIAL OF MAJOR ARMSTRONG
BY
ROBIN ODELL

ISBN 186992892x

Contains a wealth of documents and photographs

'The case of Major Armstrong, the celebrated Hay Poisoner, the only solicitor ever to hang, is one of those classic, old-fashioned English murders which hail from the heyday of courtroom drama when, with the hangman lurking in the pine-and-panel wings and the black cap an object of horrifyingly alarming currency rather than mere symbolism, the loser in 'the black dock's dreadful pen' lost all.   It comes straight out of the pages of George Orwell's essayed nostalgia ['Decline of the English Murder' in *Tribune*] for the era of the Great British Murder, when, after a Sunday lunch of roast beef and Yorkshire, you put your feet up on the sofa and, with a good strong cup of mahogany-brown tea, read all about the latest 'good' murder in the *News of the World*. And the Armstrong case was unquestionably one of the best; right up there in the grand tradition of Dr Palmer of Rugeley, Neill Cream, Mrs Maybrick, Dr Crippen, Seddon, and George Joseph Smith.'

- RICHARD WHITTINGTON-EGAN

JACK THE RIPPER
IN FACT AND FICTION

BY

ROBIN ODELL

NEW AND REVISED EDITION

Publication Date:
Autumn 2008

A Must Read
for All Ripperologists!!

Available from all good bookshops and online from
www.mandrake.uk.net
or by post
Mandrake of Oxford
PO Box 250, Oxford, OX1 1AP, UK
Phone orders (01865) 243671